Thou, Lord my allotted portion, thou my cup,
thou dost enlarge my boundaries:
the lines fall for me in pleasant places.
(PS 16:5-6 NEB)

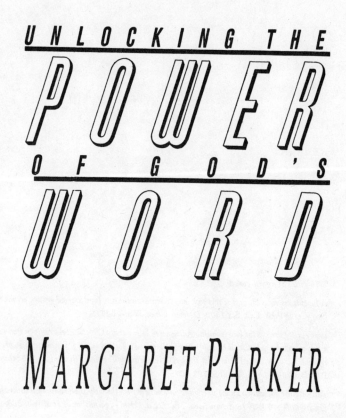

UNLOCKING THE POWER OF GOD'S WORD

MARGARET PARKER

INTERVARSITY PRESS
DOWNERS GROVE, ILLINOIS 60515

InterVarsity Press is the book-publishing division of InterVarsity Christian Fellowship, a student movement active on campus at hundreds of universities, colleges and schools of nursing. For information about local and regional activities, write Public Relations Dept., InterVarsity Christian Fellowship, 6400 Schroeder Rd., P.O. Box 7895, Madison, WI 53707-7895.

All Scripture quotations, unless otherwise indicated, are from the Holy Bible, New International Version. Copyright © 1973, 1978, International Bible Society. Used by permission of Zondervan Bible Publishers.

Cover photograph: Robert McKendrick

ISBN 0-8308-1722-0

Printed in the United States of America ∞

Library of Congress Cataloging-in-Publication Data

Parker, Margaret, 1942-
    Unlocking the power of God's word/by Margaret Parker.
      p.   cm.
    ISBN 0-8308-1722-0
    1. Bible—Criticism, interpretation, etc. I. Title.
  BS511.2.P36 1991
  220.6—dc20   90-21513
                                     CIP

14	13	12	11	10	9	8	7	6	5	4	3	2	1
01	00	99	98	97	96	95	94	93	92	91			

Acknowledgments

People think of writing as a solitary occupation, but this book has been more like a community project. In fact, many different groups have contributed to its development. The project was born in the academic community of New College Berkeley, and I am grateful to the professors there, particularly Joel Green and Francis Andersen, for the guidance and encouragement they gave me. A circle of writer friends, among them the members of the Diablo Valley Christian Writers Group, provided patient and perceptive critiquing through repeated revisions of the manuscript. Members of other small groups and classes over the years served as cooperative guinea pigs while I experimented with various imaginative approaches to Scripture.

Special thanks go to Vivian and Terry McIlraith who organized and hosted the group that field-tested the material in this book. Also crucial to the completeion of the project were those precious friends who prayed with me through the emotional ups-and-downs of the writing process.

The list of people who helped me on this book is so long that

I've hesitated to name names for fear of leaving someone out who ought to be included. But I must mention the three people whose support meant more to me than anyone else's: Bill, my husband (and computer consultant), Karin, our daughter, and Ernest Giffen, my father. They've been cheering on my writing efforts for many years. What fun it is to be able to say thanks to them in the pages of this book!

Preface

God won my heart through the power of words—the words of
the British writer C. S. Lewis. When I came back to the church
in my late twenties, desperately searching for peace and meaning, a new friend loaned me *The Lion, the Witch and the Wardrobe.*
Soon I was devouring every book by Lewis I could get my hands
on. The lively, incisive writing in his nonfictional works challenged my mind, but it was the imaginative worlds Lewis created in his fantasies that captured my heart. Through these stories, God gently wooed me back to a faith I thought I had left
behind in college.

While Lewis's words showed me a God I could love and worship, I resisted bowing to the authority of God's Word. My
childhood in a liberal church, and later studies at a liberal college, had taught me the Bible was full of silly superstitions that
no intelligent person could possibly "swallow whole." But since
Lewis and my newfound Christian friends insisted the Bible
was true, I began to grapple with Scripture, taking classes and
reading commentaries to help me grasp its meaning.

As months of study stretched into years, I became convinced

that the Bible was the inspired Word of God. However, when I actually sat down to read the Bible, it often left me bored or confused. This frustrated me. If almighty God was speaking in this book, shouldn't reading it bring me excitement and pleasure? Shouldn't I be able to exclaim, with the psalmist, "Oh, how I love your law! . . . How sweet are your promises to my taste" (Ps 119:97, 103)?

I knew it wasn't just my newness to the faith or my liberal church background that caused me to struggle with Scripture. Many of my friends who were long-time evangelical Christians admitted that they didn't really enjoy reading the Bible either. While they acknowledged its truth and power, they were glad to let preachers, Sunday-school teachers, and authors of Christian books and Bible studies tell them what the Bible said. For myself, I returned again and again to Lewis's fantasies. Somehow when I met Christ as a great lion in the Narnia stories or took a bus trip to heaven in *The Great Divorce*, I found inspiration and spiritual nourishment that I couldn't seem to find in Scripture.

Gradually God showed me a way out of my dilemma. He showed me I could read much of his Word as I had been reading Lewis's fantasies—the Bible was packed with marvelous stories and stirring poetic language. But why did it take a literature lover like me so long to tune into the literary power of Scripture?

I suspect that I failed to find the drama and action, the beauty and emotional force which pulse through the pages of Scripture because no one taught me to look for them there. The classes I attended and the commentaries I consulted led me to view the Bible as a textbook or instruction manual. I read it looking for historical facts, theological concepts and practical guidelines for living. I found what I was looking for, but I missed the sense that God himself was speaking to me, that the words of the Bible contained his life and carried his power to touch and change me.

What we find—and what we miss finding—in any endeavor is largely determined by what we go looking for and how we go about looking. Imagine two people interested in a particular stretch of wilderness in the magnificent Sierra Nevada mountains of California. One is a developer who hopes to build a ski resort. The other is a backpacker hiking the mountain trails for recreation. These two will "read" the same area quite differently.

The developer will do lots of background study, poring over maps and charts and statistical tables, learning all he can about such things as topography and weather patterns. He may fly over the area in a helicopter, noting where an access road could be built, where ski slopes might be located, where a lodge and condos would fit. All the time he will be asking himself, Does this area meet my needs?

The hiker will temporarily settle into the wilderness. She will waken to see the early morning sun setting the tips of granite peaks on fire. She will bathe her feet in icy streams and listen to the wind moving in the fir branches. Not looking for anything in particular, she just wants to experience the mountains. As she does, their beauty and peace will gladden her heart and quiet her soul.

Our society encourages a style of reading more like the developer's approach than the backpacker's. In this "Information Age" we are bombarded with enormous amounts of data. When confronted with the "required" reading that we must get through to function in our workaday world (texts, memos, instructions, news reports), we naturally skim over the material, analyzing overall patterns, identifying the central ideas. We only focus on details that will be useful to us. This seems the logical approach to take with any "serious" reading.

At times we may adopt a different reading style. We'll get caught up in a novel or a human-interest story. Like the backpacker, we will become absorbed in the world the words create rather than standing back, assessing and analyzing. However, in our fast-paced world we save this kind of reading for summer days at the beach or the minutes just before we turn off the light at night. We call it "light reading," or even "escapist entertainment."

It's not surprising I spent years studying the Bible locked into the serious-reading mode. The way society taught me to approach important reading material and the passionate commitment of the evangelical church to the importance of Scripture blinded me to the possibility that God's Word could be as gripping as a good novel, as moving as a beautiful poem.

Not that my studious, information-seeking approach to Scripture was worthless. I learned that the Bible is a complex book, a collection of many kinds of literature reflecting different historical periods, different languages and different cultures. Gathering data about various biblical genres, about the original languages, about the historical context and the theological implications of what I read, gave me a better understanding of Scripture. But understanding was only part of what I wanted and needed. Where was the joy, where was the inspiration, where was the new life I expected to find in Scripture? Only belatedly did I discover that, for me, these things could not be found in the Bible unless I was willing to come to this book less like the conscientious student and more like the little child absorbed in a favorite bedtime story.

This, I am convinced, is the way all of us ought to read the Bible—at least part of the time. I have written this book to share this way of reading, a way to get into the essentially literary character of the Bible that will unlock the power hidden there. This is not the only valid way to read Scripture. But it is an approach which, sadly, has been neglected in our time.

Only as we learn to enter into God's Word like the backpacker, opening our senses and emotions to the biblical world and surrendering ourselves in our reading, will we be challenged, refreshed and transformed. Ultimately this approach will prove to be the very opposite of "escapist entertainment." It is the kind of Bible reading that will plunge us into the very heart of reality, bring us face to face with God, let us see ourselves as we truly are, and empower us to discern and follow the path God has for us.

He who forms the mountains,
*   creates the wind,*
*   and reveals his thoughts to man,*
he who turns dawn to darkness,
*   and treads the high places of the earth—*
*   the Lord God Almighty is his name. (Amos 4:13)*

1
God Gives Us Himself in His Word

*T*he Lord God Almighty," says Amos, "reveals his thoughts to man." Can we grasp what this means? The maker and ruler of the universe, almighty God, lets us in on his thoughts and feelings. This is a privilege we humans seldom grant to each other. We rarely have the courage to put into words what we really think and feel. Instead we fill the spaces between us with careful chatter, shallow words that hide our inner selves. But the Lord God Almighty has revealed his thoughts to us. In the pages of the Bible he has "bared his soul" before his human creatures.

We must get this truth through our heads: the Bible is an intensely personal book, the words a loving heavenly Father speaks to his wayward human children to call them back to himself. We may read the Bible looking for information about God and ourselves, about history, about how to live successfully. The

Bible does give us this information. But it is not principally an abstract philosophical treatise on the nature of God and Humanity. It is not principally a dry history text crammed with facts to memorize about people long dead. It is not principally an instruction manual outlining helpful guidelines for living. At heart it is more like a personal letter or a face-to-face conversation. When we read it as God intended, we will not see cold words on a flat page. We will see the great high God stooping low to look us in the eye or whisper in our ear. For God's chief purpose in giving us the Bible was not to give us information; it was to give us himself.

God wants to give us himself, and he wants to give us new life. God means for us to be changed when we encounter him in his Word. He has spoken not just to love us but to judge us, not just to comfort us but to challenge us. Through the words of the Bible God will take hold of us, pull us closer to him, make us more like his Son. The Bible does more than convey facts. It wields power, the power of its divine author to personally make us new.

One chapter in the Old Testament, Isaiah 55, expresses for me what Scripture is all about. The prophet addressed these words to God's people, the Israelites, to encourage and challenge them as they languished in exile in Babylon. But the message of the chapter is timeless, not only conveying the specific words God meant those people to hear, but embodying the nature and purpose of all of God's Word, the whole canon of Scripture.

The chapter communicates personally; God himself speaks in all but two verses. The opening verses of Isaiah 55 reveal the anguish of God's heart. The people he loves have turned away from him and are suffering the tragic consequences of their sinfulness. God pleads with them:

> *Come, all you who are thirsty,*
>> *come to the waters;*
> *and you who have no money,*
>> *come, buy and eat!*
> *Come, buy wine and milk*
>> *without money and without cost.*
> *Why spend money on what is not bread,*
>> *and your labor on what does not satisfy?*
> *Listen, listen to me, and eat what is good,*
>> *and your soul will delight in the richest of fare.*
> *Give ear and come to me;*
>> *hear me, that your soul may live. (Is 55:1-3)*

God is asking his people to listen, to hear his words. But the emphasis is not on the kind of listening we do to comprehend certain principles or facts or instructions. The emphasis is on the kind of listening that draws us close to a person. "Come," God says in this passage, over and over. "Come to me." It's not mere words or ideas he wants to give you, God is saying, but him. "Come to me; hear me, that your soul may live." It's in knowing him that you'll find new life.

At the end of Isaiah 55, God speaks of the power his word has:

> *As the rain and the snow*
>> *come down from heaven,*
> *and do not return to it*
>> *without watering the earth*
> *and making it bud and flourish,*
>> *so that it yields seed for the sower and bread for the eater,*
> *so is my word that goes out from my mouth:*
>> *It will not return to me empty,*
> *but will accomplish what I desire*

and achieve the purpose for which I sent it.
You will go out in joy and be led forth in peace . . . (Is 55:10-12)
God is telling us that just as he has created rain with the power
to bring new life out of the earth, he has designed his word with
the power to bring new life to people's souls. He has given it to
his people so that they may be released from the spiritual thirst
and hunger, poverty and frustration referred to in Isaiah 55:1-
2. Having heard his word, his people will "go out in joy and be
led forth in peace."

This book is about how to unlock and release the power that
God has built into his Word, the power to bring us into relationship with him and to make us new people. To a great extent, the
power of Scripture resides in the kind of language it employs; our
ability to unlock that power depends on knowing how to recognize, read and respond to that kind of language.

Ordinary Language versus Literary Language

We may assume that if we are literate and can read English, we
will be able to read effectively any good English translation of the
Bible. However, this assumption fails to recognize that there are
not only different languages—English, Chinese, Greek—there
are different *kinds* of language. Within any given language, the
same words can be used differently to accomplish different purposes. Linguists use impressive technical terminology to identify
the many different ways language operates, but for our purposes
it is only necessary to distinguish between two basic kinds of
language—ordinary language and literary language. The Bible is
largely written in literary language. Since literary language func-
tions differently than ordinary language, we must learn to read
it differently.

Perhaps the best way to define the difference between ordinary language and literary language is to give an example of each. My family loves to camp, so on summer vacations we take along a guide to campgrounds. A typical entry in that book might read:

EAGLE CREEK CAMPGROUND is located in the Trinity National Forest, 12 miles north of Trinity Center via Highway 3. Terrain is forest and mountains at 2800 foot elevation. The campground is open from May 1 to October 15. There are 30 tent sites and 15 RV sites which accommodate trailers up to 16 feet long. There are pit toilets. The closest grocery store is 5 miles away. Recreational activities include fishing in Eagle Creek and the Trinity River, and berry picking.

Contrast this entry from a campground guide with the following excerpt from *A Wider View* (Diablo Valley Christian Writers Group, 1986) by Ruth Ray, an elderly friend of mine who had wonderful memories of vacations with her husband.

I stumbled out of the tent into snappy air so fresh and clean I felt it to the bottom of my lungs. Tall pines and sharp mountain peaks were pleasing to my eyes; ages of soft pine needles pampered my feet ...

Soon coffee, bacon and a sharp crackling fire combined with pungent forest scents to make what must be the most irresistible fragrance in the world. Music came from the little stream as it burbled and rippled its cheerful way over the rocks.

This was our favorite place of refreshment. Spirit, soul, and body let down into deep silences; fresh sights and sounds reminded us of God's abundance and variety; the newness of morning called us to listen and lift our hearts before Him.

The first of these examples is ordinary language; the second is literary language. The differences between the two are summarized on the following chart.

Ordinary Language:	Literary Language:
is used to inform us	is used to involve us in experience
gives us knowledge about the subject matter	lets us relate to the subject matter, know it personally
we read asking, "What can I get out of this?"	we read asking, "How can I get into this?"
holds the material at a distance, helping us analyze it	leads us to surrender to the material, letting it take hold of us

In a sense, ordinary language is more useful and efficient than is literary language. If I enjoy camping and am trying to decide which campground to visit, the campground guide will give me the information I need to narrow my choices. If my family is on the road, it's late afternoon, and the kids are hungry, bored and fighting in the back seat, the guide will show us the nearest campground where we can stop with our fifteen-foot trailer to spend the night.

Literary language is not so concerned with practical information. My elderly friend's description does not tell me the elevation of the camping spot or instruct me in building a campfire. Instead it lets me experience camping as the writer experienced it. I can enter imaginatively into the sights and sounds, the smell and feel of camping. I can share the thoughts and emotions of the writer as she revels in the special world of pines and peaks. Her words do not tell me how to camp, but they may make me want to go camping.

The chief function of literary language is to let us participate in experience, to get us involved on several levels. While ordinary language relays facts or concepts which we can process with our rational faculties alone, literary language engages our senses, feelings and imaginations, as well as our intellects. Ordinary language and literary language may both speak about the same subject matter, and both do convey ideas or information. But literary language contains certain elements which go beyond informing us to touch us, stretch us, transform us.

The verses of Isaiah 55 quoted earlier are written in literary language. As we look more closely at these verses, we will see how the prophet's words work to grab hold of us and involve us in experience. The passage grips us at the level of our senses, emotions and imaginations because it uses imagery, drama and analogy.

Imagery, Drama, Analogy

Imagery is one of the most powerful tools literary language uses to involve us. *Imagery* is simply any language which appeals directly to our senses—which helps us see, hear, smell, taste or feel what is being talked about. The Isaiah passage captures our attention immediately with the reference to thirst, a basic sensation we all feel. Subsequent references to food—wine and milk and bread—build to a promise that "your soul will delight in the richest of fare." These phrases appeal to all the senses that eating appeals to: taste in particular, but also smell and sight and a sense of satisfied fullness. As the passage proceeds, the imagery changes to that of weather and agriculture. The prophet's carefully chosen words make us feel the cool wetness of rain and snow falling from heaven, make us see the wonder of green plants budding and flourishing.

In addition to imagery, this passage contains human *drama*. The essence of drama is that it gives us real people in situations we can relate to and makes us care what happens to them. Drama usually involves some kind of conflict. In Isaiah 55, we can glimpse the internal conflict that churns within the Israelites whom God is addressing. These people are empty, frustrated people, people who are hungry for something but can't find fulfillment, people who work hard to make themselves happy but remain dissatisfied. Their desires and expectations are never quite met by their achievements and acquisitions. We can relate to these people and their internal conflict because all of us at one time or another have felt a gnawing sense of unmet desire.

The passage also gives us a picture of God that we can relate to, even identify with. The pleading words this God speaks express how much he loves these frustrated, unfulfilled Israelites. He is feeling frustrated too, for he has repeatedly offered his people just what they need—himself and his word—yet they ignore him and plod along their own illusory paths to happiness. "Why?" he asks them. "Why spend . . . your labor on what does not satisfy?" If we have ever loved someone who is hurting, repeatedly reached out to help them, yet had them reject our help and go their own destructive way, we can feel with God his hurt and longing in this passage.

The personal conflicts in Isaiah 55—conflicts within the hearts of the rebellious people, conflicts between themselves and their loving God—draw us into a drama, and we wonder what the conclusion will be. Will the people learn that God is the only food that can fill their deepest hunger? Will God's loving heart be satisfied as his people turn to him? We find ourselves rooting for God to have his way. If he can draw the people close, all the conflicts will be resolved. God, his people, indeed all of creation will be satisfied. As the passage closes, God gives a picture of a future time when the conflicts will be resolved, when the people

> . . . *will go out in joy*
> *and be led forth in peace;*
> *the mountains and hills*
> *will burst into song before [them],*
> *and all the trees of the field*
> *will clap their hands. (Is 55:12)*

This promise of a happy ending touches and thrills us as readers because we have identified with the frustrations and disappointments of the people and God. This sharing in human emotions, this getting caught up in conflict and longing for resolution, is what gripping drama is made of.

Besides imagery and drama, a third literary element plays a crucial role in the Isaiah passage. This element, *analogy* or *metaphor*, is one of the most powerful ways that literary language grabs our imaginations and helps us participate in experience. While ordinary language tries to say just what it means, using precise words in a literal way, literary language often invites us to compare what is being talked about with something else. That "something else" is not the real subject under discussion, but it is introduced because it can help us understand the subject in a deeper, broader way.

God's real subject in Isaiah 55 is the distance between his people and himself and his desire to draw them close. However, the people he is addressing have hardened their hearts and denied their need for him. If he speaks to them directly of their spiritual bankruptcy, they will not be moved. Physical want, on the other hand, is a concrete experience they understand and fear; one of their problems is that they depend on the earthly, the material, to satisfy their needs. So God hits them at the level of their worldly anxieties, speaking of thirst and hunger and poverty to jolt them into recognizing the spiritual crisis they are in.

Not only is spiritual need expressed metaphorically as physical need. Spiritual fulfillment is identified with earthly fulfillment. God is promising that the souls of his people will live if the people draw close and listen to him. But he entices them to pay attention by picturing this new spiritual life in terms of earthly pleasures and rewards. Verse 2 promises that listening to God will be as satisfying as eating a sumptuous meal. Verses 10-11 use images of a rich harvest to express the new life to be found in God's presence.

The Isaiah passage demonstrates beautifully how the three basic elements of literary language work together to involve us in experience. Isaiah's imagery activates our senses as we visualize (or hear, taste, feel or smell) what is being described. The human drama in the passage plays on our emotions as we empathize with people like ourselves and with a personal God caught up in circumstances we can relate to. And the prophet's analogies stretch our imaginative capacity as we stop to wonder how our souls are like arid land or empty stomachs, how God's words are like rain or snow or a banquet.

The adjoining chart summarizes how literary language works.

Why God Speaks in Literary Language

How do you react to the literary language of Isaiah 55? Do you wonder why God doesn't just "say what he means," why he doesn't speak more simply and directly? It may be difficult for you to believe, but there are good reasons why God uses literary language to communicate with his human creatures. Once we recognize these reasons, we can feel even more grateful for the gift of his Word.

God's principal reason for speaking to us is to give us himself,

IMAGERY	activates our SENSES	as we VISUALIZE (or hear, taste, smell or feel) what is described.
DRAMA	arouses our EMOTIONS	as we EMPATHIZE with the people in the passage.
ANALOGY	captures our IMAGINATION	as we SYNTHESIZE, discovering the hidden likenesses in two unlike things being compared.

to let us know him more and more intimately. Yet how can we know God intimately? He is the Almighty, the ruler of heaven and earth. A vast gulf looms between him and his creatures. God reminds us of this in Isaiah 55.

"For my thoughts are not your thoughts,
neither are your ways my ways,"
declares the LORD.
"As the heavens are higher than the earth,
so are my ways higher than your ways
and my thoughts than your thoughts." (Is 55:8-9)

The only way the gulf can be bridged is for God to reach down to us. He must speak a language that, like rain and snow, originates in heaven but can descend to our level. He must speak a language that our earthbound natures can take in. So, more often than not, God uses literary language, a language of imagery and human drama and analogies to things we experience in this world. As we have seen, Isaiah 55 abounds with examples of such language, but I will point out one more. In verse 11 God speaks of the word that goes out from his mouth. Is God saying that he has a literal mouth? No, but he has a great desire for us to draw close to him and experience his love, and to do that we need to be able to picture him in human terms.

In a sense, Scripture is parallel to the Incarnation. Just as God's Son laid aside his heavenly glory to become like us and to be with us, so God must somehow take his thoughts and feelings, which are far beyond us, and present them at our level. The Bible is not humans using human language to grasp God, for we never can grasp God. The Bible is God using human language to grasp us, to give himself to us, at least as much of himself as we are capable of taking in. His book must be like a child's picture book, a book of images and human drama and analogy, or else the spiritual realities God wants to convey could never be meaningful to us.

Not only does God intend that the Bible should help us know him. He also intends that it should help us know ourselves. Unless we can see how needy, self-centered and self-deluded we are, we will never draw close to God. Therefore God's words, like rain and snow which soak into the thirsty ground, must have the power to penetrate into our very souls. We need to be changed at many levels. Only part of what needs changing, perhaps a rather small part, is at the intellectual level. Much of our sin resides in our flesh and feelings, in the unconscious ways we have of looking at things or refusing to look at things. Imagery, drama and metaphor can reach us at these deeper levels; ordinary language may change our minds but have little impact on our hearts.

The people who produce advertising in this Information Age know what kinds of communication have power to change our behavior. Commercials do not stick to logical, straightforward arguments to sell their products. In fact, they rarely present much factual information. Instead they rely on images to catch our eye, music to move us, characters and drama to arouse our emotions. All these speak to deep desires in us that we may not even acknowledge. We then buy the product on the basis of these desires (though we may try to rationalize our purchases with logic).

I am not saying that God ignores our intellect. The literary sections of Scripture are not simply images and feelings devoid of content. They mean something. They convey true information about God, humanity and salvation, and that information reaches our minds as the other elements speak to other levels of our being. Furthermore, there are parts of Scripture (particularly the legal sections of the Old Testament and the epistles of the New Testament) where the language used is more often ordinary than literary.

Even in the midst of the very poetic language of Isaiah 55, there is a brief section which employs more ordinary language. This section is spoken not by God, but by his prophet.

Let the wicked forsake his way
  and the evil man his thoughts.
Let him turn to the LORD, and he will have mercy on him,
  and to our God, for he will freely pardon. (Is 55:7)

Here the prophet articulates in relatively unimaginative language God's demand for repentance and his promise of reconciliation. But God apparently does not expect blunt language by itself to move his people. If he did, why would he have surrounded it with vivid analogies that point out the people's plight and with concrete pictures of the pleasures they will experience when they draw close to him? In Scripture God is the consummate advertiser. Because he knows that nothing can satisfy people like a relationship with himself, he uses the power of words to persuade them to "buy into" new life with him. So great is his love for people that he is willing to woo them. For wooing he needs literary language, the kind of language that can touch their hearts.

Why We Fail to Respond

If literary language has the power to move us and change us, why do we so often read the Bible and remained unchanged? Sometimes the simple truth is that we do not want to change. We are purposely holding God at arm's length even as we read his Word. But often we come to the Bible hungry for God, hoping to meet him and be remade by him, yet we cannot find him in the words on the page. We miss him and his transforming power because we do not know how to read the literary language he uses.

Many of us have little practice reading imaginatively. When we want to experience the pleasure of story or drama, we turn to films or television. Because these forms of storytelling actually give us pictures and sound rather than relying on words to capture our senses and arouse our emotions, we don't need to use much imagination to enjoy them.

A further barrier to our responding appropriately to literary language is the way our culture has taught us to read. As I discussed in the preface, we learn from school and work that serious reading needs to be analytical and objective. Imaginative involvement in what we read is only for novels and other recreational reading. We forget that the most serious reading we will ever do, the reading of God's Word, is meant to be recreational in the true sense, re-creating us and giving us new life. The literary language in Scripture calls us to read imaginatively, with a kind of mental playfulness. But because we take the Bible so seriously, we feel it is somehow sacrilegious to read it this way.

Ironically, even the way the church has taught us to read the Bible may have hindered our ability to respond to Scripture. Because the Bible's authority has come under serious attack in the last two centuries, those who cherish God's Word have often tried to defend it by insisting that it can and must be read like a science textbook or a logical philosophical treatise. Such people inform us that we must carefully and respectfully extract the historical facts, the essential doctrines and the clear instructions from Scripture. We must never read our own subjective experience into it.

Yet God himself, by choosing to speak in literary language, has invited us to come to our Bible reading subjectively. He has invited us to bring our senses and emotions and imaginations into play. Each of us has the capacity to read the Bible this way, but this capacity has probably been lying dormant. It needs to be nudged awake.

Waking Up to the Literary Power of Scripture

The chapters that follow are intended to sensitize you to the pervasive presence of literary language in the Bible. Each chapter focuses attention on a particular category of imagery or drama. You will see how various motifs—pictures of animals, for example, or courtroom scenes—appear over and over in Scripture. Soon you'll realize that a reader must be on the lookout for such language, not only in the Bible's poetry and narratives but in every kind of biblical literature.

While you are getting a taste of the abundance and variety of the literary language God uses in his Word, you'll also be learning basic principles that help you respond appropriately to such language. The chapters demonstrate reading approaches that allow you to get caught up in the Bible's literary power, but they also suggest precautions you can take to avoid getting carried away in wrong directions.

Every chapter is followed by a brief Bible study. These studies help you tune into passages that feature the same kind of imagery or drama highlighted in the preceding chapter. If you're like me, when you come to these "exercises" you'll be tempted to skip right over them and get on with reading the book. But you'll be missing out on the chance to experience familiar Scripture in fresh ways—responding when Jesus speaks in the Gospels, hearing the mood music behind a psalm, laughing with Paul when he cracks a joke, visualizing John's vision of heaven on the screen.

The studies after each chapter are fun to do, but they have a very serious purpose. You are reading this book to learn to participate imaginatively in God's Word, yet a studious, analytical approach to the Bible probably comes as naturally to you as breathing. The best way to break out of old reading habits is to practice new ones. The exercises at the end of each chapter let you practice.

As you read through this book, try out new ways of responding to the images and drama in the Bible. You may discover more excitement and enjoyment in reading Scripture than you have ever experienced before. More important, you will be opening yourself to God, the God who wants to relate to you personally and change you radically through the power of his Word.

When God Speaks:

A Bible Study Focused on
Selected Passages from Scripture

Please note: The questions in this study do not have right and wrong answers. Since literary language appeals to our senses, emotions and imaginations, our responses to the power of such language are necessarily personal. Answer the questions honestly, not the way you think you should answer them.

The quotations in this study are drawn from different versions of the Bible to remind you that using more than one version often helps us tune into the literary language in Scripture.

1. Below are four passages about God speaking to his human creatures and their response to him. Go through the passages one at a time, answering the following questions for each passage: Does the language appeal to your senses? Which ones? Does the passage engage your emotions? How? Does the passage stimulate your imagination? In what way?

Exodus 19:9, 17-19 (New International Version)
The LORD said to Moses, "I am going to come to you in a dense cloud, so that the people will hear me speaking with you and will always put their

trust in you." . . . Then Moses led the people out of the camp to meet with God, and they stood at the foot of the mountain. Mount Sinai was covered with smoke, because the LORD descended on it in fire. The smoke billowed up from it like smoke from a furnace, the whole mountain trembled violently, and the sound of the trumpet grew louder and louder. Then Moses spoke and the voice of God answered him.

Psalm 19:7-10 (King James Version)
The law of the LORD is perfect, converting the soul: the testimony of the LORD is sure, making wise the simple. The statutes of the LORD are right, rejoicing the heart: the commandment of the LORD is pure, enlightening the eyes. The fear of the LORD is clean, enduring for ever: the judgments of the LORD are true and righteous altogether. More to be desired are they than gold, yea, than much fine gold: sweeter also than honey and the honeycomb.

Psalm 50:16-17, 21 (New English Bible)
God's word to the wicked man is this:
   What right have you to recite my laws
and make so free with the words of my covenant,
   you who hate correction
   and turn your back when I am speaking? . . .
All this you have done, and shall I keep silence?
   You thought that I was another like yourself,
but point by point I will rebuke you to your face.

Luke 8:4-8, 11 (Revised Standard Version)
And when a great crowd came together and people from town after town came to him, he said in a parable: "A sower went out to sow his seed; and as he sowed, some fell along the path, and was trodden under foot, and the birds of the air devoured it. And some fell on the rock; and as it grew up,

it withered away, because it had no moisture. And some fell among thorns; and the thorns grew with it and choked it. And some fell into good soil and grew, and yielded a hundredfold. . . . Now the parable is this: The seed is the word of God."

2. Read the following verses from the epistles which talk about how God's Word affects us.

2 Timothy 3:16-17 (New American Standard Bible)
All Scripture is inspired by God and profitable for teaching, for reproof, for correction, for training in righteousness; that the man of God may be adequate, equipped for every good work.

Hebrews 4:12 (Good News Bible)
The word of God is alive and active, sharper than any double-edged sword. It cuts all the way through, to where soul and spirit meet, to where joints and marrow come together. It judges the desires and thoughts of man's heart.

Put each of these two passages in your own words. In what way are they saying much the same thing? Which passage was easier for you to paraphrase? Why?

3. If ordinary language is defined as language whose main purpose is to convey information, and literary language is defined as language that invites us to participate in experience, where would you place each of the six passages you just read on the scale below?

Ordinary Language   **Literary Language**

4. Of the six passages you have read in this study, which one spoke most forcefully to you personally? Why?

5. We speak of having a personal relationship with God and with Jesus Christ. We might also think of ourselves as having a personal relationship with God's Word. How would you define your relationship with the Bible?

For example, you might say, "The Bible and I got together often when I was growing up, but we haven't been in touch for several years" or, "The Bible is like a mother to me. It always understands where I'm coming from and says just the words I need to hear."

6. Are there any changes you would like to make in your relationship to the Bible? What are they?

Why then have these people turned away? . . .

Each pursues his own course
   like a horse charging into battle.
Even the stork in the sky
   knows her appointed seasons,
and the dove, the swift and the thrush
   observe the time of their migration.
But my people do not know
   the requirements of the LORD.
How can you say, "We are wise,
   for we have the law of the LORD,"
when actually the lying pen of the scribes
   has handled it falsely? (Jer 8:5-8)

2
Letting God's Language Move Us

W*e can hear the frustration in God's voice as he*
speaks the words of Jeremiah 8:5-8 to the citizens of Judah
through his prophet. What is the matter with these people? Over
and over again God has demonstrated his love for them and has
told them clearly what he expects from them. They have his law.
In fact, their scribes study it and write about it, and pride themselves on their understanding of it. Yet they haven't really heard
what God has told them. Instead they go their own way like
headstrong animals. It is clear to God that even birds with their
tiny brains follow his will better than his chosen people do.

Communication that doesn't connect—we all experience it.
The father explains to his son the destructive consequences of
his misbehavior, but the explanation only seems to make the
behavior more appealing to the boy. The wife tries to tell her
husband how much she loves him and needs him, but he resents

what he perceives as her efforts to control him. The boss writes out instructions that clearly define the procedures his employees are to follow, but they mess up the job anyway.

The problem is, it takes two to communicate. The speaker tries to put his thoughts and feelings, perceptions and desires into the words he says. The person who listens brings to the task of listening his own thoughts and feelings, perceptions and desires. The result may be that the listener hears something very different from what the speaker is trying to say.

Communication between people is not simple or easy. The same can be said for communication between God and humanity. God could have made us robots or animals and programmed into our brains only the paths and connections that would mirror his own mind. (Presumably the migration routes of birds are somehow programmed into their brains like this.) But instead he gave us minds of our own. He wanted us to be able to think and reason, feel and imagine as he does, so that we could freely choose to love him and live in fellowship with him.

Since Adam and Eve used the freedom God gave them to choose to disobey their Creator, we humans have a sinful tendency to act in ways that are contrary to God's ways. But though we may behave like unruly animals, we are still people created in God's image, and God will not violate our personhood by forcing our allegiance. With his might he could easily defeat us and destroy us, but might will not win us over to his side; love cannot be coerced. To win us God uses a gentle weapon, the weapon of the Word.

God's Word is powerful, but it cannot overpower us. Remember, it takes two to communicate. No matter how true or forceful God's speech is, its effect depends in part on how we listen. It does no good for God to be communicative if we are not receptive. Our challenge in reading Scripture is to know what we must bring to the communication process in order to hear truly what God wants to say to us.

Exegesis and *Eisegesis*

Several years ago I took a class in hermeneutics, the study of how to interpret Scripture correctly. I can clearly remember the professor writing two words on the blackboard: *exegesis* and *eisegesis*. The first word, he explained, referred to the right way of reading Scripture. We should approach the Bible objectively, with open minds, getting out of it only the meanings God had built into the words, being careful not to read in any prejudices or presuppositions of our own.

The second word, *eisegesis*, was almost a "dirty word" in the eyes of my teacher. It referred to the unfortunate tendency of many people to read into Scripture things that were not there. He warned us to beware of the personal biases and desires that could color our reading. If we allowed these subjective responses to play a part in biblical interpretation, we would twist God's words to mean what we wanted them to mean and thus undermine the power of the text to convey God's true message to us. "What does it mean to me?" was the last question we should ask as we read the Bible.

The professor's ideas made a lot of sense to me. We humans, with our sinful bent, are always in danger of misreading God's Word, hearing what we want to hear. Clearly, this was the situation Jeremiah was addressing in the quotation that opened this chapter. The scribes of Judah, the very people whose profession was to study and interpret God's law, were handling it falsely, and the people were happy to accept their false interpretations. According to my hermeneutics class, the proper antidote for this mishandling of divine truth would have been for the people of Judah to lay aside their personal biases and motives and to listen to God's word objectively and studiously. Then they could have heard God correctly.

However, God did not send his willful people a hermeneutics professor to teach them to listen to God with scholarly caution. He sent them the prophet Jeremiah, who spoke to them in some of the most emotional, impassioned language in all of Scripture. His oracles were packed with imagery, drama and analogy which could powerfully sway the people. But their power would depend not on the people's objectivity but on their willingness to respond personally, emotionally, imaginatively to the language.

One thing we learn from the book of Jeremiah is that in reading Scripture we need to find a middle path between the cautious objectivity my teacher taught was necessary for correct exegesis and the self-serving Scripture-twisting of eisegesis. There is a way to *read into* God's Word, to bring our personal experiences and feelings to it, which allows us to hear God's meaning more clearly, not less. In fact, when we are dealing with the literary language in the Bible, our spontaneous emotional and imaginative responses are a legitimate part of exegesis.

Of course a studious, objective approach to Scripture has its place. The painstaking work of Bible scholars has contributed greatly to our understanding of God's Word. But when our main goal is to allow Scripture to shape our lives, caution and objectivity should not be our first concern. There will be time for scholarly research after we purposely have surrendered ourselves to the power of the language.

In this chapter, the focus will be on becoming more sensitive to the kind of language in Scripture that demands a spontaneous subjective response and, then, learning what kind of personal response is appropriate. Because we will look closely at examples from the book of Jeremiah, we need to understand a bit of the background behind that book.

Jeremiah's Tough Audience

Jeremiah was a prophet to the southern kingdom of Judah. He lived through the political upheavals that finally resulted in the destruction of Jerusalem and the exile of the Jews to Babylon. For forty years, Jeremiah preached God's message to the people of Judah. He told them to expect and to accept conquest and punishment because they had turned away from him to worship idols and had committed injustices which flouted God's laws. The words God spoke through Jeremiah were most often words of harsh judgment like the following:

"Hear the word of the LORD, all you people of Judah. . . .

"Will you steal and murder, commit adultery and perjury, burn incense to Baal and follow other gods you have not known, and then come and stand before me in this house, which bears my Name, and say, 'We are safe'— safe to do all these detestable things?

From the time your forefathers left Egypt until now, day after day, again and again I sent you my servants the prophets. But [the people] did not listen to me or pay attention. They were stiff-necked and did more evil than their forefathers.

So beware, the days are coming, declares the LORD, when . . . the carcasses of this people will become food for the birds of the air and the beasts of the earth, and there will be no one to frighten them away . . . for the land will become desolate." (Jer 7:2, 9-10, 25-26, 32-34)

Though God put in Jeremiah's mouth scathing indictments of sin and dire predictions of doom, Jeremiah was as much a bearer of God's yearning love as of his burning anger. God hoped his prophet's harsh words would penetrate his people's thick skins, shatter their stiff-necked stubbornness and turn them back to himself. The Lord explained his motives to Jeremiah: "Perhaps when the people of Judah hear about every disaster I plan to inflict on them, each of them will turn from his wicked way; then I will forgive their wickedness and their sin" (Jer 36:3).

History tells us that few of the citizens of Judah really heard the words God directed at them through his prophet Jeremiah. They may have listened, but not with open minds and hearts, for they ignored, ridiculed or persecuted this prophet. However, we can tell, just by looking carefully at the word pictures Jeremiah used, what kind of listening would have led to a correct understanding and response. By highlighting a few brief passages from the book of Jeremiah, we will gain a better idea of how to read picture language whenever we meet it in Scripture. In this chapter we will focus exclusively on figures of speech involving animals.

Recognizing Imagery, Analogy and Symbolism

Most of us have vague—and not necessarily pleasant—memories of learning terms like *simile, metaphor, imagery* and *symbol* in English class. Though we don't need to know the technical names for various literary strategies in order to be moved by them, becoming alert to these figures of speech is one good way to heighten our sensitivity to the power of literary language. Jeremiah alone provides us with hundreds of examples of word pictures ranging from straightforward images to subtle symbols.

An example of pure imagery may be seen in Jeremiah's description of a drought in Judah, a drought God brought upon the land to punish the people's sinfulness.

> *The ground is cracked*
> *because there is no rain in the land;*
> *the farmers are dismayed*
> *and cover their heads.*
> *Even the doe in the field*
> *deserts her newborn fawn*
> *because there is no grass. (Jer 14:4-5)*

This is pure imagery because Jeremiah's words painted a literal picture of the reality they were describing.

Jeremiah often combined imagery with obvious analogies called *similes.* The two passages below employ similes, the first comparing the rebellious nation of Judah (God's "inheritance") to a lion, the second comparing God himself to a lion.

> *My inheritance has become to me*
> *like a lion in the forest.*
> *She roars at me;*
> *therefore I hate her. (Jer 12:8)*

> *The peaceful meadows will be laid waste*
> *because of the fierce anger of the LORD.*
> *Like a lion he will leave his lair,*
> *and their land will become desolate. . . . (Jer 25:37-38)*

Sometimes Jeremiah used metaphors. These are figures of speech which, instead of using "like" or "as" to make a comparison, simply identify one thing with another. In the following verses the prophet compared the idolatrous people he was addressing with animals in heat, but instead of saying to them,

"You are *like* animals," he said, "You *are* animals."

"How can you say, 'I am not defiled;
I have not run after the Baals'? . . .
You are a swift she-camel
running here and there,
a wild donkey accustomed to the desert,
sniffing the wind in her craving—
in her heat who can restrain her? . . .
You said, 'It's no use!
I love foreign gods,
and I must go after them.' " (Jer 2:23-25)

We immediately recognize that when imagery is combined with analogy, the words must be read figuratively, not literally. God is not much like a lion who lives in a lair, and the people of Judah could never be mistaken for roaring lions or lustful camels and donkeys. Nevertheless, the power of literary analogies lies in the fact that there is some meaningful resemblance between two essentially unlike things. Our imaginations then play with the comparison to discover just how many similarities we can find.

Jeremiah sometimes combined imagery not with analogy but with symbolism. While an analogy is not meant to be read literally, a symbol does make a literal reference to the thing it names, but it also carries other, larger meanings with it. The cross is a powerful symbol. It does refer to the literal, concrete instrument of Christ's execution, but it also points to larger truths about God's forgiving love and man's callous sinfulness, about the defeat of Satan and the reconciliation of humans with their Maker.

There was an example of symbolism in the quote that opened this chapter:

Even the stork in the sky
knows her appointed seasons,

    and the dove, the swift and the thrush
      observe the time of their migration.
    But my people do not know
      the requirements of the LORD. (Jer 8:7)

The stork, dove, swift and thrush are birds which do migrate through Palestine on a seasonal basis, and Jeremiah wanted his audience to think first of actual birds when they heard these lines. It is apparent, however, that the prophet was using migrating birds to point to a larger truth: it is natural and beautiful for all God's creatures, even the simplest, to follow his laws. Jeremiah made the birds a symbol of obedience.

Imagery, analogy and symbol may shade into each other or be so intertwined that they are not easy to sort out. Nevertheless, understanding the different ways they work, and knowing when to read literally and when figuratively, can protect us from confusion and misinterpretation as we read God's Word. Having recognized them, however, we will find there is still much more to do before we can feel the full impact of a literary passage.

Mining Rich Language

Words are often rich with meaning. They do not travel light, but are loaded down with baggage, carrying around with them not only their dictionary definitions but a generous supply of associations. Words often have a kind of mood or atmosphere about them; even words which have the same basic meaning can evoke very different mental pictures and feelings. *Steed* and *nag* both refer to horses, but the first word radiates energy, nobility and spirit, while the second is weighed down with associations of homely decrepitude. The words *donkey* and *burro* refer to the same beast, but we probably think of the first as the epitome of stubborn orneriness, while the second seems lovable and appealing.

Writers who want to help us participate in what they experience delight in using words laden with overtones and undercurrents of meaning. They will choose images that have particular associations for them, hoping that these images will call up similar associations for their audience. Thus anytime we encounter literary language, we are being invited to bring to its words the experiences and emotions that cluster around them in our own minds. This is one way the language personally involves us.

Where do we get our associations for various words? Some seem to be universal, growing out of the very nature of the thing named. Some associations are cultural. Some may be highly personal associations arising from an individual's unique experiences.

If we ask ourselves where we acquired the associations that cluster around various animal names in our minds, we will see they have many sources. Animals seem to hold a special fascination for us from infancy on. Though they cannot speak, animals occupy some of our earliest lessons in language (the dog says, "Bow wow"; the pig says, "Oink, oink"). Probably nursery rhymes, fairy tales and other children's books were a major influence on our developing ideas about animals. Certainly television programs featuring animals had their effect on most of us. In addition, some of our associations may be based on memories of farm animals or family pets. (The word *rat* began to carry new connotations for me when my daughter acquired a lively, likable little rodent as a pet.)

In the passage about the drought from Jeremiah 14:1-7, we can see how the prophet conveyed his message by using animal images that carry powerful and predictable associations. Among the images Jeremiah used to describe the drought, he included a doe and a fawn. Deer have sympathetic associations in our minds. Of all animals, they are among the most lovely, graceful and delicate. They are shy and easily frightened, for they do not prey on other animals but are preyed on. Hence deer (especially newborn fawns) convey a sense of innocence and defenselessness, and we are particularly moved by their suffering. Furthermore, Jeremiah's wording exploits all the sentimental feelings we have for mothers and babies. When we read the description of a doe deserting her fawn in the midst of the drought, this arouses many of the same emotional reactions the Walt Disney film *Bambi* evoked in us when the wild animals fled before the raging forest fire, when the fawn's mother was killed by a hunter's bullet.

Jeremiah wanted to impress on the people of Judah how tragic and unnatural the drought was. He began by describing how people in the cities and on the farms were suffering from the lack of rain. But it was the picture of the doe and fawn that Jeremiah finally counted on to hit home with his audience. He knew that the drought was God's judgment on the people for their backsliding. By showing them that their sin had brought tragedy not just on themselves but on the loveliest and most innocent of God's creatures, he hoped to arouse in them a sense of shame and loss that would turn them back to God.

Associations also heighten the impact of Jeremiah's words in the passage about migrating birds. He reminded his listeners that "the dove, the swift and the thrush observe the time of their migration. But [God's] people do not know the requirements of the Lord." Undoubtedly part of his intent was to ridicule their rebelliousness, saying, in effect, "You stupid people! Even 'birdbrains' know enough to obey God. Why don't you?" But the prophet could have chosen any animal with remarkable instinctive behaviors (ants, for example) to make this point. Why did he choose birds as symbols of obedience to God's laws? The answer may lie in the powerful associations birds carry for us.

Birds are natural, universal symbols of joyous freedom. Seeing them fly, we dream of soaring as they do above the earth. They seem an unlikely choice as symbols of obedience. And yet they may be the perfect choice to symbolize obedience to God: in obeying God, people can find a surprising freedom they have never known before. By using birds to illustrate obedience to God, Jeremiah was in a sense holding out a promise to his listeners, a promise of the new life they could enjoy if they would only surrender again to God's will. Jeremiah's symbolism may have been an effort to woo the stubborn people back to God by appealing to the same longings in them that birds in flight arouse.

While Jeremiah probably hoped to call up in his listeners all their sympathetic associations for does and fawns and all the desires for freedom that birds in flight can evoke, a writer will not always want to make use of all the associative baggage a word carries. This was clearly the case when Jeremiah spoke of Israel as "a swift she-camel running here and there" and "a wild donkey accustomed to the desert." These images occur in the midst of a moving oracle in which God was telling his chosen nation that, though he had loved and cared for her as a bride, she had prostituted herself by worshiping idols. When Jeremiah compared his listeners to camels and donkeys in heat, he was forcefully reminding them of how far they had fallen and how much they had lost. As God's cherished bride, they could have continued in a loving, trusting relationship with him. Instead, by indiscriminately pursuing the favors of false gods, they had relinquished not only their precious position with God but their true humanity as well.

Jeremiah's audience would have had many positive associations with camels and wild donkeys, beasts which were highly valued in their society. Camels were used as beasts of burden and were important sources of milk, wool, and other products. Wild asses were considered a hunter's prize, for they were larger and stronger than domestic donkeys.[1] Elsewhere Jeremiah pictured both animals in sympathetic terms (Jer 14:6; 49:32). But for obvious reasons Jeremiah did not want to evoke these positive associations when he spoke of camels and donkeys in relationship to Judah's apostasy. Such associations would have diluted rather than enhanced the power of his message. So he focused very explicitly on the animals' mindless, unrestrained mating behavior, leaving his hearers in no doubt about the point he was making.

Rich Language Is Risky

Writers are not always so careful to spell out which associations they want us to bring to words. Quoted earlier were two passages containing similes involving lions. Lions have had symbolic significance throughout history. (Currently lions serve as the logo for a motion-picture company, as the Christ-symbol in C. S. Lewis's "Chronicles of Narnia," and as the name of a professional football team, among other things.) Lions carry a variety of associations. We think of them as noble, fearless, commanding, rightfully called the king of beasts. We think of them as ferocious, bloodthirsty, heartless hunters and killers. We think of them as lithe, swift, beautiful felines, poetry in motion as they pursue their prey.

Let's look at two lion similes Jeremiah used and ask what associations we should bring to them.

Like a lion [God] will leave his lair,
    and their land will become desolate

because of the sword of the oppressor
and because of the LORD's fierce anger. (Jer 25:38)

My inheritance [Judah] has become to me
like a lion in the forest.
She roars at me;
therefore I hate her. (Jer 12:8)

When a lion image is used to represent an angry God, should our focus be on God as a ferocious, fearsome destroyer, or does the picture invite us to read in overtones of majesty, even of beauty? Are associations of courage and power, lordliness and agility appropriate when we read that rebellious Judah is like a lion? Or did Jeremiah really mean to portray Judah as a pathetic creature who was all roar and bravado, skulking in the forest hiding from God, the real King of beasts? Your responses may not be the same as mine; neither of us can be sure our interpretations are the ones the prophet intended.

Rich language, the language of imagery, analogy and symbol, is often risky language. Because figures of speech purposely exploit the overtones of words, the multiple shades of meaning they carry with them, we must read literary passages looking for more than simple dictionary definitions. We must ask what the words make us think, how they make us feel. Yet if we bring too many associations to a figure of speech, we can muddy its meaning. If we make the wrong associations for any given word, we may miss the meaning entirely.

We may think we can avoid the risk of misinterpretation by conscientiously keeping our own subjective responses out of our reading. But rich language loses its power when we try to hold it at a safe distance. It demands that we dwell in it richly and let it dwell in us richly (see Col 3:16).

Any writer who counts on calling up personal associations and emotions in readers takes the chance of being misunderstood. In the case of Scripture, it was God himself who took this risk: he gave us a book full of literary language. This language does not always make it easy for us to keep our facts straight or our theology neat. Rather, it is the kind of language that can penetrate our personalities and transform us.

God spoke to the people of Judah through the vivid language of Jeremiah because he yearned to transform them. Perhaps the picture of birds in flight could capture the people's imaginations and turn them back to their Creator. Perhaps the image of the dying doe and fawn could bring tears of remorse that would melt their stony hearts. Unfortunately, those who heard Jeremiah did not open themselves up to his language. They would not yield to the power of God's words. They willfully rebelled, and God called them "foolish and senseless people, who have eyes but do not see, who have ears but do not hear" (Jer 5:21).

Sadly, our failure to hear and respond to God is often due to our mistaken conviction that we must read the Bible objectively, with scholarly caution. The book of Jeremiah clearly demonstrates that we must not read literary language that way. We need to be willing to risk opening ourselves to the power of Scripture. God wants us to be moved by his Word.

Beasts of Burden:

A Bible Study Focused on Animal Imagery

Matthew 11:28-30

1. If you had to characterize yourself as a specific animal (or bird or insect), which animal would you choose? (Example: "I keep as busy as a beaver" or "I'm a mother hen.") In what ways are you like this animal? What are some characteristics we associate with this animal that you do not think apply to you?

Please note: In the Gospels Jesus often uses animals figuratively to represent people. The most frequently used metaphor compares people to sheep. But in Matthew 11:28-30 Jesus speaks of people not as sheep, but as beasts of burden, or draft animals, yoked to pull plows or carts. Since these jobs were usually performed by donkeys or oxen in first-century Palestine, these are the animals Jesus undoubtedly had in mind when he spoke these words.

2. Read Matthew 11:28-30 aloud from three different versions of the Bible. What do Jesus' words make you see, feel, hear, smell or taste? Which of your senses do these verses appeal to most strongly?

3. Have you ever been in circumstances where you felt like a beast of burden or draft animal? Recall that experience. How easily can you relate to the animal metaphor used here?

4. How do you react to Jesus picturing his followers as work animals? Does the comparison comfort you? Challenge you? Offend you? Why?

5. What clues in the passage indicate that people are not just like animals, even though Jesus compares them to oxen and donkeys? What indications are there that Jesus is not like a typical master?

6. In what ways have you felt that your relationship to Jesus has placed a yoke on you? In what sense has that yoke proved to be restful, easy, a burden that is good to bear?

7. Read the parable in Luke 15:3-7 in which Jesus uses a sheep analogy. In what way does this passage convey the same truths Jesus taught in Matthew 11:28-30? What different insights do we gain by seeing ourselves as donkeys or oxen rather than sheep?

8. Do you prefer to see yourself as a sheep, or as an ox or donkey? Why?

9. Read Matthew 11:28-30 as Jesus' personal invitation to you now. Imagine the tone of his voice, the expression on his face as he speaks. Write out, as honestly as you can, the response you feel toward this invitation.

God's voice thunders in marvelous ways;
    he does great things beyond our understanding. . . .
He loads the clouds with moisture;
    he scatters his lightning through them.
At his direction they swirl around
    over the face of the whole earth
    to do whatever he commands them.
He brings the clouds to punish men,
or to water his earth and show his love. (Job 37:5, 11-13)

If he holds back the waters, there is drought;
    if he lets them loose, they devastate the land. (Job 12:15)

_____

3
Context Channels Our Responses

W*ater is the most common substance on earth and* one of the most essential. Appropriately, water imagery can be found almost everywhere in Scripture. How should we respond to this pervasive imagery? Is water our friend or our enemy? Is water cause for rejoicing or terror? Is water the source of growth or destruction? It is all these things and many more. As the writer of Job reminds us, it's hard to know what to think about water. Not enough of it is a bad thing; too much of it may be worse.

The water images in Scripture speak with great power, but not necessarily with great precision. As the last chapter pointed out, most word pictures carry rich, varied, even contradictory associations. Water is a particularly versatile class of imagery. The biblical writers pictured water in many forms—from dew to hail, from rivulets to flash floods. And they demonstrated that water has dramatically different effects—from nurturing crops to wiping out armies.

Because water is such a slippery image, capable of carrying

multiple associations and arousing diverse emotions, focusing on water imagery will help us answer a question raised by the last chapter: In trying to enter into literary language and hear it speak to us personally, should we allow our imaginations free play? Should we let them call up any and every connotation the words carry in our minds? Is tuning into the Bible's imagery essentially a process of free association?

The answer is no. Images in the Bible are not like inkblots that we can view and interpret any way our individual personalities dictate. Rather, each word picture in Scripture appears in a specific context. It is part of a sentence, paragraph or stanza, and it is also part of a larger literary unit—a historical narrative perhaps, or a letter or lyric poem. The context always suggests the kinds of associations we can legitimately bring to an image. Naturally, the writer will not try to spell out all the helpful associations for each image. That would leave no room for the kind of personal responses that literary language nurtures. But the context in which the writer places each image will channel our responses to it.

Reading images as if they were separate inkblots would be an exercise in self-analysis or self-expression. We would be shaping God's Word to fit our own personalities. But God intends his Word to shape us. Surrendering ourselves to the power of his Word means, among other things, reading its images *in context*. The Bible is put together in such a way that its words will move us in the direction God desires.

Reading Images in Their Immediate Context
Below are several brief quotes, each containing one or more water images. Drawn from various books of the Bible, they provide a small sampling of the powerful ways water imagery is used

both literally and figuratively in Scripture. As you read these quotes, note how the imagery divides into two distinct categories. Certain kinds of water images consistently carry positive associations. Other kinds are usually negative.

Positive Water Imagery

O Lord, you preserve both man and beast.
How priceless is your unfailing love! . . .
you give [men] drink from your river of delights.
For with you is the fountain of life. (Ps 36:6-9)

The streams of God are filled with water
to provide the people with grain,
for so you have ordained it.
You drench its furrows
and level its ridges;
you soften it with showers
and bless its crops. (Ps 65:9-10)

With joy you will draw water
from the wells of salvation. (Is 12:3)

Then will the lame leap like a deer,
and the mute tongue shout for joy.
Water will gush forth in the wilderness
and streams in the desert.
The burning sand will become a pool,
the thirsty ground bubbling springs. (Is 35:6-7)

Then the angel showed me the river of the water of life, as clear as crystal, flowing from the throne of God and of the Lamb down the middle of the great street of the city. (Rev 22:1-2)

Negative Water Imagery

For forty days the flood kept coming on the earth, and as the waters increased they lifted the ark high above the earth. . . . Everything on dry land that had the breath of life in its nostrils died. (Gen 7:17, 22)

The LORD is a warrior;
the LORD is his name.
Pharaoh's chariots and his army
he has hurled into the sea.
The best of Pharaoh's officers
are drowned in the Red Sea.
The deep waters have covered them;
they sank to the depths like a stone. (Ex 15:3-5)

My soul is downcast within me;
therefore I will remember you
from the land of the Jordan,
the heights of Hermon—from Mount Mizar.
Deep calls to deep
in the roar of your waterfalls;
all your waves and breakers
have swept over me. . . .
I say to God my Rock,
"Why have you forgotten me?" (Ps 42:6-7, 9)

But the one who hears my words and does not put them into practice is like a man who built a house on the ground without a foundation. The moment the torrent struck that house, it collapsed and its destruction was complete. (Lk 6:49)

Become mature, attaining to the whole measure of the fullness of Christ.
   Then we will no longer be infants, tossed back and forth by the waves, and blown here and there by every wind of teaching and by the cunning and craftiness of men in their deceitful scheming. (Eph 4:13-14)

These excerpts are very brief. We would normally want to read more than this—at least a full paragraph or stanza—in order to respond appropriately to any word picture. Yet even the few phrases surrounding each water image above clearly suggest the kinds of association the writer wants that image to carry. The river and fountain pictured in Psalm 36 embody God's love, which brings life and delight to his creatures. The deep waters of the Red Sea in the Exodus account mean defeat, terror and death for Pharaoh's soldiers.

Sometimes our personal associations for particular images will run counter to the way they are used biblically. If I were to read Psalm 42's references to waterfalls, waves and breakers apart from the context, my associations would be positive. I would remember hikes to Yosemite's awesome waterfalls, weekend getaways to the scenic northern-California coast, relaxed days of beachcombing on Kauai's north shore. These vacation memories call up times when I felt especially close to God and delighted in the beauty of his creation.

However, the flow of Psalm 42 tells me that positive associations like these were foreign to the psalmist's intentions. For him, the thought of waterfalls, waves and breakers simply aggravated his feelings of despondency and distance from God. A commentary helps me understand that the writer viewed these cataracts so negatively because they were on the slopes of Mount Hermon, far from the temple and city he loved. Probably an enemy army had carried him into exile there.[1]

Surrendering to the biblical images *in their context* means that I let the negative pictures of water in Psalm 42 catch hold of my imagination and shift it toward personal associations that reinforce the writer's meaning rather than undermine it. Therefore, reading that the psalmist's soul was downcast at the sound of Hermon's waterfalls, I recall the time I stood at the top of Vernal Falls in Yosemite, with no protective barrier between me and the torrent, seeing and hearing tons of water hurtling over the brink. I had to fight back a sense of terror, for the current seemed strong enough to draw me in and drag me over the edge to my destruction. That memory helps me enter into the despair expressed in Psalm 42. I can feel, with the writer, the waves of loneliness and depression that are washing over him and dragging him down emotionally.

As the biblical writers brought their personal feelings to the words they wrote, so we must bring our feelings to the words if they are to speak to us. But we shouldn't attach associations to the words haphazardly. Rather, focusing attentively on images in their immediate context allows us to hear truly the meanings God has built into them. When I listen to Psalm 42's water images in context, I hear God reminding me that loneliness and depression are real, powerful emotions that even God's people must experience. God understands these feelings and wants us to bring them to him. He will not judge us; he will bring healing to our spirits.

Seeing Images in Their Larger Context

Images do not draw their meaning solely from the particular

poem, narrative or other literary unit in which they appear. Frequently they belong to larger patterns of imagery that weave their way throughout the Bible. As we read in widely scattered parts of Scripture, it is fascinating to see these larger patterns emerge. We realize that writers who lived in many different centuries and wrote in many different genres often used the same kinds of imagery in startlingly similar ways. This shouldn't surprise us when we remember that they were all inspired by the same God and were contributing to the telling of one great divine-human drama; God designed his Word so that many of its repeated images bear a consistent message from Genesis to Revelation. Reading images in context means we will be aware not only of their immediate surroundings but of the larger context, the way they speak in the Bible as a whole.

The passages quoted earlier demonstrate that much of the biblical water imagery divides into two broad streams of meaning: positive and negative. The positive category includes pictures of rivers, streams, springs, pools, fountains, wells, dew and rain. In the Bible these images are tied repeatedly to all God's good gifts, bountiful harvests and the quenching of physical thirst, as well as gifts of salvation, healing, peace, God's Word, the Holy Spirit and life itself. In contrast, images of deep waters—seas and lakes with their waves, and rivers and streams in flood—usually are associated with evil, danger, judgment and death.

The way the biblical writers used these various forms of water imagery makes sense if we understand their geographical and cultural environment. Rain and dew, rivers and streams, springs and wells naturally had positive associations for those who lived in the arid Near East. People who had to expend great effort to obtain and conserve the water needed for themselves and their livestock appreciated every source of fresh water.

On the other hand, these people were aware of the dangers of deep water. The Israelites, though not a seafaring people, fished the Sea of Galilee where treacherous storms often arose. They understood that merchants and fishermen might wrest a living from deep waters, but only at great risk. And they knew that even their life-giving streams could carry sudden death when a heavy downpour resulted in flash floods in the desert riverbeds. Such a flood is pictured in Psalm 124:

If the LORD had not been on our side
  when men attacked us,
when their anger flared against us,
  they would have swallowed us alive;
the flood would have engulfed us,
  the torrent would have swept over us,
  the raging waters would have swept us away. (Ps 124:2-5)

Many twentieth-century Americans will not relate readily to the biblical writers' strong feelings about water. When we can turn on a faucet or sprinkler system and have all the fresh water we want, we may think of this precious commodity as common and dull. Conversely, many of us associate the ocean and lakes not with terror and destruction but with recreation. It is, then, more on a theoretical level that we understand how essential fresh water is to life and how dangerous deep-water activities (even fun ones like surfing and scuba diving) can be. What modern Americans will undoubtedly find hardest to identify with are the supernatural associations ancient peoples brought to deep waters.

People in Bible times often viewed seas and lakes as the residing places of monsters and demons; the ocean was the very embodiment of chaos. Pagan cultures in the Near East had myths which pictured the world being created when God struggled with a sea monster. By slaying the monster, God established order, and by creating dry land he held the chaos of the deep waters in check. Old Testament writers repeatedly borrowed this mythical conception when they sought a dramatic way to picture God's creative and redemptive powers.

> *But you, O God, are my king from of old;*
> *You bring salvation upon the earth.*
> *It was you who split open the sea by your power;*
> *you broke the heads of the monster in the waters.*
> *It was you who crushed the heads of Leviathan*
> *and gave him as food to the creatures of the desert.*
> *It was you who opened up springs and streams;*
> *you dried up the ever flowing rivers. (Ps 74:12-15)*[2]

We almost certainly hear echoes of the ancient mythology in the creation account in Genesis 1. The "deep" and the "waters" with which the account opens represent primordial chaos, but God's hovering Spirit is seen imposing order on the chaos as the waters are commanded to take their proper place.

In New Testament times, deep waters were still viewed as the habitat of God's adversaries, of demons and of Satan himself. When Jesus healed the Gadarene demoniacs and the demons were sent into a herd of pigs, the demon-possessed pigs immediately rushed into the Sea of Galilee and were drowned (see Mt 8:31-32). When Jesus miraculously stilled a storm on the lake and saved his disciples' lives, Mark says the disciples were afraid after the waves died down. "Who is this?" they asked each other with terror in their voices (Mk 4:41). It is quite possible that the disciples viewed Jesus' calming of the waves not so much as evidence of his power over natural forces as proof of his ascendancy over the demonic.[3]

In the visions of Revelation 12 and 13, Satan appears as a dragon who tries to destroy the Christ child and his mother by drowning them in a torrent of water that spews from its mouth. When this attempt fails, the dragon's ally, a fearsome beast, emerges from the sea to rule the wicked, persecute the saints and blaspheme God. Again deep waters are tied to the demonic, to evil and death. This pattern continues in John's vision of the final judgment, though here the deep-water imagery is combined with fire imagery to represent judgment:

> *The sea gave up the dead that were in it, and death and Hades gave up the dead that were in them, and each person was judged according to what he had done. Then death and Hades were thrown into the lake of fire. The lake of fire is the second death. (Rev 20:13-14)*

Watching an image pattern repeat itself in Scripture affects us much like hearing a theme with variations recur in a great symphony. Each time the image appears, it has greater power to move us.

For example, individual pictures of deep waters acquire more ominous overtones and undercurrents when we read them in the whole biblical context. John's description of the new heaven and the new earth at the end of Revelation includes the simple phrase "there was no longer any sea" (Rev 21:1). This may seem an enigmatic, even anemic, image until we recall all the other biblical references to deep waters. Then we realize the phrase, "there was no longer any sea," is actually a powerful symbolic assertion of God's victory over Satan and death, over all the forces of fear, evil and destruction in the world.

Similarly, positive water images build in power as we see them repeated in Scripture. Jesus tells the woman at the well, "Whoever drinks the water I give him will never thirst. Indeed, the water I give him will become in him a spring of water welling up to eternal life" (Jn 4:14). The woman can't take in the wonderful implications of Jesus' promise. She replies, "Sir, give me this water so that I won't get thirsty and have to keep coming here to draw water." But as we recall all the uplifting water imagery in the Psalms and Prophets, we understand that a spring of water from God means much more than the quenching of physical thirst. Jesus is offering the woman—and us—salvation, new life, healing, joy, peace, the Holy Spirit, and the gift of fruitful living in God's everlasting kingdom. All this is bundled up in Jesus' image of "a spring of water welling up to eternal life."

The Immediate Context Is the Key

Even though many images are enhanced when we recognize their place in the whole biblical tapestry, we must not consider the larger context more important than the immediate context. If we focus on each water image we meet in the Bible, we quickly learn we cannot read water images as if they were some kind of predictable code: wells = refreshment, waves = death, rains = blessing. In the quotes which opened this chapter, all the water images did fit the traditional patterns. But water imagery—and most imagery, for that matter—is flexible. In the quotes below, writers have chosen to use images of a well, the sea and rain in ways that do not fit the traditional biblical scheme.

> *"This city must be punished;*
> *it is filled with oppression.*
> *As a well pours out its water,*
> *so she pours out her wickedness.*
> *Violence and destruction resound in her." (Jer 6:6-7)*

> *Shout for joy to the LORD, all the earth,*
> *burst into jubilant song with music; . . .*
> *Let the sea resound, and everything in it,*

the world, and all who live in it.
Let the rivers clap their hands,
*   let the mountains sing together for joy. (Ps 98:4, 7-8)*

Lacking clothes, [the poor] spend the night naked;
*   they have nothing to cover themselves in the cold.*
They are drenched by mountain rains
*   and hug the rocks for lack of shelter. (Job 24:7-8)*

These examples remind us that the immediate context should be the first place we look for the intended meaning of any given image. We can think of the immediate context as a channel that guides our memories, emotions and associations in the direction God desires. We may discover, however, that similar images from elsewhere in Scripture flow like tributaries into that same channel, swelling its force and increasing its depth so that God's Word can speak to us with added power.

Ultimately, the power images hold for us as individual readers depends on our willingness to pour our own personal experiences into the flow of the literary language. As we allow our feelings, memories and longings to mingle with those of the biblical writers, the Bible will play a larger role in shaping our imaginations and directing our actions. We will be like the one described in Psalm 1 who, "meditates day and night" on Scripture, and is compared to "a tree planted by streams of water." As we thrust our roots, all the complex elements of our lives, down into the nourishing, life-giving stream of God's Word, we will grow as God desires and yield fruit in season.

The Images of Psalm 46
We close this chapter with a look at Psalm 46, one of the best-

loved psalms in all the psalter, because this psalm contains strong water imagery in its first two stanzas.

God is our refuge and strength,
* an ever present help in trouble.*
Therefore we will not fear, though the earth give way
* and the mountains fall into the heart of the sea,*
though its waters roar and foam
* and the mountains quake with their surging.*

There is a river whose streams make glad the city of God,
* the holy place where the Most High dwells.*
God is within her, she will not fall;
* God will help her at break of day.*
Nations are in uproar, kingdoms fall;
* he lifts his voice, the earth melts. (Ps 46:1-6)*

The water imagery here follows the usual biblical pattern: destructiveness represented by the deep waters of the sea, blessing represented by a river. Still, the psalm holds some surprises. We will appreciate those surprising images more fully when we are sensitive to both their larger biblical context and their immediate context.

In the first stanza, the imagery of mountains falling into the heart of the sea apparently pictures the action of an earthquake, but it is a quake of startling dimensions. We have the sense that the solid land is being taken over by the sea, that the mountains themselves have become like surging water. When we view such imagery in the light of the larger literary tradition of Scripture, its full impact comes into focus. We remember that the Bible writers sometimes drew on ancient mythology and pictured God creating the world by taming the waters and establishing the solid land over them. Here the poet seems to be visualizing the opposite process, with the chaotic sea swallowing up the land. Perhaps the ultimate undoing of the whole created order is darkly glimpsed here.[4] Through this imagery, the psalmist asserts that even in circumstances that seem like "the end of the world," God can be trusted.

In the second stanza, the scene shifts from mountains in the ocean to a river in a city. To appreciate the force of the river image we need to focus on the context created by this and the following stanzas. That the poet is picturing the chaotic conditions of wartime is suggested in the words, "Nations are in uproar; kingdoms fall." The use of the fortress image and references to bows, spears and shields in the following verses all reinforce this theme of war.

Once we have discovered that the context is war, the picture of the city in the second stanza comes into sharper focus. Jerusalem, the "city of God," is under siege. It is night, and the darkness makes the inhabitants' fear even more oppressive; the enemy may attack at daybreak. In our imaginations we can empathize with the terror of God's besieged people.

Into this context of wartime chaos, the poet inserts the picture of "a river whose streams make glad the city of God." Just as he wrested the greatest possible impact from the destructive water imagery of the first stanza, he manages here, through context, to effectively highlight the crucial life-giving role of water. The inhabitants of a besieged city know how precious water is. If they are cut off from a fresh-water supply, surrender to the enemy will soon be the only alternative to death by thirst. But if they have a free-flowing river in their city, they can hope to hold out and ultimately triumph. Thus in this single image the poet captures a sense of all the good things God provides in times of trouble.

Ultimately the psalm calms and comforts by assuring us God is in control, no matter how chaotic the circumstances may seem. If any "unmaking" is to be done, God will do it: "He lifts his voice, the earth melts" (v. 6). If desolation occurs, it is God's desolation (v. 8). In the meantime, God's people know they have God's presence and, with it, all the blessings symbolized by a river flowing in God's city.

Knowing the larger biblical context can enhance our appreciation of the ocean imagery in stanza one; recognizing the immediate context of wartime helps us feel the full impact of the river image in stanza two. But we should pause here to note that even though our understanding of context is important, God can manage to communicate much through the power of images alone.

God used Psalm 46 to quiet my heart and help me learn to trust him long before I became aware that the end of the world might be glimpsed in stanza one and that war was the underlying context of the whole psalm. The picture of mountains falling into the ocean always gave me a sense of trouble so terrible that I knew God could easily handle my small problems. The lyrical description of streams that "make glad the city of God" never failed to calm and comfort me, even though I did not recognize the significance of fresh water in a besieged city.

Often the imagery of the Bible has the power to carry us in the right direction emotionally and intuitively—even when we do not understand it fully. This should encourage us in our reading. For sometimes the context will be confusing, and even the commentaries we consult may not agree on the meaning. Nevertheless, the images of Scripture are so vivid, so elemental, they can begin to touch and move us as soon as we come to them with eager minds and open hearts.

Raging Waters, Glad Streams:

A Bible Study Focused on Water Imagery

Psalm 46

1. Read Psalm 46 aloud from three or more versions of the Bible.

2. Verses 2-3 give a startling description of catastrophe. When you read these words, what do you see? hear? feel?

3. Have you ever had an experience with water in any form that helps you identify with the frightening picture painted in verses 2-3? Describe that experience.

4. What crisis in our present world or in an individual's life might verses 2-3 represent? Where do you see something crumbling which had appeared, like the mountains, to be solid, stable and dependable? What forces of destruction and chaos threaten, like the surging sea, to undermine the solid foundations of life?

5. Verses 4-5 have a tone which contrasts with that of the surrounding portions of the psalm. If you were setting the whole psalm to music, how would verses 4-5 sound? How would the other portions of the psalm sound?

6. In terms of military strategy, a river in a besieged city would be a source of fresh water enabling the city to hold out against the enemy. Here the river is a metaphor for any resource which God may make available to his people in a time of trouble. What resources does the river image make you think of?

7. Do you personally find the river image to be an effective metaphor for God's presence and help? Why or why not? What are some different biblical pictures you like to call to mind to reassure yourself of God's care for you?

8. When your world seems to be crumbling around you, or when you feel under attack, how do you usually respond? In what ways is the response Psalm 46 calls for different from your usual response?

9. Have you ever experienced the peace expressed in verses 4-5, not because God removed you from trouble but because you felt his presence in the midst of it? Try to recall the details of that experience.

10. Right now, what trouble (ranging anywhere from minor to major) threatens your peace? In verse 10 God says to us, "Be still." How does Psalm 46 help you to "be still" in your present trouble?

When I turned, I saw . . . someone "like a son of man," dressed in a robe reaching down to his feet and with a golden sash around his chest. His head and hair were white like wool, as white as snow, and his eyes were like blazing fire. His feet were like bronze glowing in a furnace, and his voice was like the sound of rushing waters. In his right hand he held seven stars, and out of his mouth came a sharp double-edged sword. His face was like the sun shining in all its brilliance.

When I saw him, I fell at his feet as though dead. Then he placed his right hand on me and said: "Do not be afraid." (Rev 1:12-17)

4
Can We Take Some Imagery Too Seriously?

T *he words of Revelation 1:12-17 describe Christ as the* apostle John saw him in a vision. The passage, bursting with imagery, seems to invite us to visualize Jesus just as John must have seen him. While we can picture a figure with a long robe and a golden sash around his chest, we soon run into trouble. Can we really imagine Jesus with eyes like blazing fire, a mouth with a sword coming out of it and a face like the sun?

A pastor who was teaching a course on Revelation some years ago announced that this passage made Christ sound weird. Since we all knew that Christ wasn't weird, his advice was not to take the imagery of these verses literally. I'm sure many people in the class breathed a sigh of relief when he said that; trying to visualize this passage just did not make sense. When they put together in their mind's eye all of John's descriptive phrases, from Jesus' snow-white head to his molten feet, the result was a ludicrously surreal picture of their Lord that they simply could not take seriously.

In this chapter we will focus on several passages which feature images of the human body, which are used in such startling ways that we aren't quite sure how to respond. We may be tempted to ask, "Can I really be expected to take such imagery seriously?" And as we look at the passages highlighted, we will discover that all biblical imagery does not call for the same approach. Creativity and common sense are needed to discern which approach works best with any given image.

What If Images Cannot Be Visualized?

Previous chapters have stressed the importance of responding directly with our senses to the imagery in Scripture. In our matter-of-fact society we often miss much of the power of literary language because we are too quick to translate poetic images into abstract ideas. Therefore, we are wise to ask of every image we meet, "What picture does this call to my mind? Can I imagine how it would be to hear, smell, touch or taste what is being described?" However, we need to be aware that some biblical imagery is more symbolic than sensuous, more abstract than concrete. When images do not engage our senses directly, we may need to find another way to read them.

This is the case in Revelation 1:12-16. Our common sense and the surrounding literary context tell us that John intends to give us a sublime picture of Christ. Since visualizing John's images produces a bizarre picture of Jesus, we need to try another approach.

Although John's images do not add up visually, the words carry associations that do add up emotionally. The picture of Christ's head and hair being white like wool or snow conveys a sense of purity and innocence, reminding us of Christ's moral perfection. When the next clause mentions the blazing eyes of Jesus, we feel the gaze of our sinless Lord burning into us, uncovering every sin. Further images of heat and light (Christ's feet like glowing bronze, his face like the sun) intensify our sense of standing exposed before a Savior who would purify and refine us. Reference to Christ's voice like rushing water reminds us of the flood imagery in Scripture that represents God's judgment on sin; the picture of the sharp double-edged sword coming out of Jesus' mouth calls to mind the Hebrews passage about God's living word penetrating our souls and laying bare our hidden thoughts. Reading all these images for their emotive, symbolic impact instead of their visual impact, we can no longer consider them ludicrous. They are awe-inspiring and convicting.

By tuning in to the emotional impact and symbolic significance of the imagery in Revelation 1:12-16, we can experience a sense of the potent purity of the risen Lord. At the same time we gain an awareness of our unworthiness in his presence. But we would be kidding ourselves to think we could fully grasp the meaning of these images. Surely part of the purpose behind the surreal pictures in Revelation is to overwhelm our senses, to stretch our imaginations to the breaking point. The imagery reminds us that there is no way we can completely understand who our Lord is or how he works.

John's response to Christ's appearance, falling at his feet as though dead, is an appropriate response to the overwhelming vision he has seen. But immediately following John's swoon, the picture of Jesus becomes very human. He places his hand on his disciple and says, "Do not be afraid." Here, alongside word pictures beyond our imagining, are images that are perfectly down-to-earth. We can see Jesus as a caring friend, feel his gentle hand on our shoulder and hear his soothing voice in our ear.

Apparently, there are no neat formulas for correct reading that can guide us through a passage like John's vision of Christ. Sometimes the truths that are conveyed can touch us first and very directly at the sensory level. Sometimes the images bypass our senses to stimulate emotional associations. Some images are really more like abstract symbols whose meaning needs to be explained before their impact can be felt. And we must consider one other possibility: some images may be meant to bring us to our knees mentally, reminding us that there are things we simply cannot comprehend. We need to try reading images in different ways, searching for the approach which will unlock their power.

What If Biblical Images Are Gruesome or Humorous?

Most of the images in Revelation 1:12-17 cannot be visualized without producing a ludicrous picture of Christ that actually undermines the impact of the passage. However, we should not jump to the conclusion that it is wise to ignore the direct sensual impact of all images that are shocking or amusing. God may purposely use language to horrify us or to set us laughing. In the Gospels we find Jesus using body imagery to produce both responses.

In Mark 9 Jesus gives his disciples some gruesome advice:

If your hand causes you to sin, cut it off. It is better for you to enter life maimed than with two hands to go into hell, where the fire never goes out. And if your foot causes you to sin, cut it off. It is better for you to enter life crippled than to have two feet and be thrown into hell. And if your eye causes you to sin, pluck it out. It is better for you to enter the kingdom of God with one eye than to have two eyes and be thrown into hell. (Mk 9:43-47)

Repeatedly we have heard Bible teachers explain that Jesus here is using hyperbole, a figure of speech which exaggerates for effect. Such teachers point out that of course Jesus does not expect us to follow his advice literally. Unfortunately, we may get the impression that we do not need to take the *message* seriously. But hyperbolic language does not excuse us from tuning our senses carefully to what is being said. This passage begs to be visualized.

Jesus uses body imagery to alert us to the tight grip sin has on us. His words suggest that we may be as attached to our vices as we are to our eyes, hands and feet. Parting with them will be as painful and terrifying as submitting to mutilation. Yet hell, Jesus makes clear, is far worse than any pain and terror we will experience in surrendering our sins to God.

Jesus is not above using images of bloody mutilation and ugly disfigurement to convince us to let go of the sins we love. We naturally want to sidestep the power of these images, and we can do this by casually dismissing them as hyperbole. But if we fail to see and feel and be repulsed by Jesus' horrifying pictures, we may continue to cling to the very sins which cut us off from God's saving grace.

If some of Jesus' word pictures are revolting, others can make us laugh. Take, for example, his parable about focusing on the speck of sawdust in a brother's eye when we have a plank in our own (Mt 7:3-5). Jesus is drawing a kind of cartoon for us here, and the humor is very broad. It is on a par with a television sketch in which a psychologist earnestly recommends firmer parental discipline on the part of a client while the therapist's own child can be seen wreaking havoc in his office, under his very nose. We can't help chuckling at a person who is so sure of his own rightness, so blind to his own failings.

However, we are the real targets of our laughter. How often have we stood in judgment over someone else while being guilty of far worse faults? Even as we snicker smugly at the self-right-eous fellow with the plank in his eye, we are doing the very thing Jesus' words condemn. Humor has a way of sneaking up on us, hitting home before we have a chance to avoid its uncomfortable insights. But the effectiveness of Jesus' parable depends on our visualizing his joke. It is funny—and sad—to picture a person who has to look around the log in his own eye to see the speck he's trying to remove from another's. Are we that person?

What If Images Seem to Convey Half-truths?
The two preceding examples from the Gospels make it clear that we should not shrug off images, ignoring their sensual impact, simply because the pictures they paint are horrible or funny. God may package truth in revolting or humorous ways. However, we may sometimes hesitate to take images seriously because they seem to lead us away from the truth. Don't some word pictures in Scripture actually contradict basic biblical teachings?

This is a question that may trouble us when we meet anthro-pomorphic imagery applied to God. Repeatedly in the Old Tes-tament, God is pictured with human form or qualities, with eyes and ears, hands and feet, and very human feelings and thought processes. Many people in our sophisticated society blithely dis-miss such descriptions as naive efforts of primitive peoples to fashion a god in their own image. Evangelical Christians cannot dismiss such imagery as easily, for they believe the language of the Bible is divinely inspired. Yet they may sense a real spiritual danger in taking such language too seriously. When we picture God in human terms, aren't we in a sense domesticating him by bringing him down to our level, encouraging in ourselves a false sense of parity with, or even control over, the great high God? Take, for example, the account of the creation of Adam and Eve in Genesis 2. Here God is clearly pictured anthropomorphically.

And the LORD God formed the man from the dust of the ground and breathed into his nostrils the breath of life, and the man became a living being.

Now the LORD God had planted a garden in the east, in Eden; and there he put the man he had formed. And the LORD God made all kinds of trees grow out of the ground—trees that were pleasing to the eye and good for food. . . .

The LORD God said, "It is not good for the man to be alone. I will make a helper suitable for him."

Now the Lord God had formed out of the ground all the beasts of the field and all the birds of the air. He brought them to the man to see what he would name them; and whatever the man called each living creature, that was its name. So the man gave names to all the livestock, the birds of the air and all the beasts of the field.

But for Adam no suitable helper was found. So the LORD God caused the man to fall into a deep sleep; and while he was sleeping, he took one of the man's ribs and closed up the place with flesh. Then the LORD God made a woman from the rib he had taken out of the man, and he brought her to the man.

The man said, "This is now bone of my bones and flesh of my flesh." (Gen 2:7-9, 18-23)

This is a story whose language certainly invites us to respond very directly, to enter in with our senses and to identify emotionally. Reading verses 7-9, we can almost see the intent expression on God's face as he forms Adam. We can feel the cool pliability of the clay in God's hands and sense the warm breath of God in Adam's nostrils. We can imagine the artistic pleasure the creator feels as his creation takes shape, and we can share his sense of excitement when the figure stirs and comes to life. We can guess how God delights in placing Adam in the perfect garden world he has made.

A few verses later God realizes that his creation is not yet perfect: "It is not good for the man to be alone." God brings the animals to Adam to see if any of them is a suitable companion for him. When none of them proves acceptable, God makes a woman and presents her to the man. We can imagine God's pleasure first in seeking, then in creating the perfect companion for Adam, for we too have a creative component that delights in solving problems.

We can imagine all these things—but should we? When we allow ourselves to get caught up in the imagery of Genesis 2, we tend to picture God as very human, a bigger and cleverer version of ourselves. This God has fingers and lungs and a mouth, and he solves problems by exploring various options before finding a satisfactory answer. Isn't this a dangerously misleading picture of God? Can the imagery of Genesis 2 be trusted? How seriously should we take it?

These questions arise not just with the anthropomorphic imagery applied to God in the Old Testament, but with much of the imagery in Scripture. Often biblical images seem to contradict biblical truth. And often biblical truths seem to contradict each other. Christianity is full of startling paradoxes. Particular images in the Bible sometimes may appear to mislead us because they reflect only one side of these paradoxical truths.

For example, one of the richest and most astounding paradoxes in our faith is the tension between God's transcendence and his immanence; he is at the same time beyond our control and within our reach. The anthropomorphic imagery in Genesis 2 and elsewhere may make us uneasy because it seems to highlight God's approachability at the expense of his omnipotence.

Biblical Images Keep Paradoxical Truths in Balance

While Genesis 2 does seem to present a God who is too familiar, not awesome enough, the imagery used throughout the Old Testament effectively captures the tension that exists between these two poles of truth. Anthropomorphic language does not give us the simple-minded picture of a god created in humanity's image. In fact such imagery, woven together with other imagery, manages to convey forcefully both God's transcendence and his immanence.

The following account in Exodus—couched in deceptively unsophisticated, highly anthropomorphic language—evokes God's willingness to be available to humanity as well as the awful distance that separates God from humanity.

Then Moses said, "Now show me your glory."

And the LORD said, "I will cause all my goodness to pass in front of you. . . . But," he said, "you cannot see my face, for no one may see me and live."

Then the LORD said, "There is a place near me where you may stand on a rock. When my glory passes by, I will put you in a cleft in the rock and cover you with my hand until I have passed by. Then I will remove my hand and you will see my back; but my face must not be seen." (Ex 33:18-23)

Frequently, the Old Testament writers counterbalanced the tendency of these images to make God seem too tame by mixing anthropomorphisms with imagery that identified God with the forces of nature. In David's poem below, body metaphors mingle with images of earthquake, volcano and storm as God's actions are described.

In my distress I called to the LORD;
  I called out to my God.
From his temple he heard my voice;
  my cry came to his ears.

The earth trembled and quaked,
  the foundations of the heavens shook;
  they trembled because he was angry.
Smoke rose from his nostrils;
  consuming fire came from his mouth,
  burning coals blazed out of it.
He parted the heavens and came down;
  dark clouds were under his feet.
He mounted the cherubim and flew;
  he soared on the wings of the wind.
He made darkness his canopy around him—
  the dark rain clouds of the sky.
Out of the brightness of his presence
  bolts of lightning blazed forth.
The LORD thundered from heaven;
  the voice of the Most High resounded.
He shot arrows and scattered the enemies,
  bolts of lightning and routed them.
The valleys of the sea were exposed
  and the foundations of the earth laid bare
at the rebuke of the LORD,
  at the blast of breath from his nostrils.

He reached down from on high and took hold of me;
  he drew me out of deep waters. . . .

He rescued me because he delighted in me. (2 Sam 22:7-20)

The first and last stanzas portray an accessible God, a God with ears and hands who listens and reaches out. But the intervening verses, though referring to God's nostrils, mouth and feet, make it impossible for us to forget that our Lord is a God of awesome power, sheer majesty and impenetrable mystery.

When we come to the New Testament, we no longer find body imagery applied to God. Instead he is spoken of as spirit (Jn 4:24), as the "King of kings and Lord of lords, who alone is immortal and who lives in unapproachable light, whom no one has seen or can see" (1 Tim 6:15-16). But this does not mean that the New Testament fails to give us a sense of God's immanence. The New Testament writers simply did not need to use pictures of God in human form to help us experience his closeness to us and identification with us. They could give us pictures of Jesus himself, God in the flesh come to live among us.

In the Gospels we see Jesus taking little children in his arms (Mk 10:16), touching the bodies of the diseased (Mt 8:3), stripping off his clothes to wash his disciples' feet (Jn 13:4-5). Here is a Savior whose pierced hands and wounded side we can touch when our faith is weak (Jn 20:27), whose feet we can kiss and wet with our penitent tears (Lk 7:38).

And yet, the Gospel portrayals of Jesus keep a balance too. He is not only God in his closeness, but God in his majesty and terrible might as well. He is fully, literally human; yet the disciples see him walking on water and see him transfigured in brightness on a mountainside. These manifestations of Jesus' divine nature in the Gospels have much the same effect as the Old Testament descriptions of God riding the storm or shining like the sun. Whether we look at the pictures painted by the language of the Old Testament or the New, we cannot escape the tension between God's transcendence and his immanence.

We are foolish to dismiss the anthropomorphic descriptions of divinity in the Old Testament as naive. Quite the contrary, they foreshadow the Incarnation, that ultimate complex mystery that lies at the heart of our faith. Exactly how perfect God and perfect man could coexist in our Lord Jesus Christ is beyond understanding. Nevertheless, we rejoice in the pictures in Scripture that help us experience this paradoxical truth.

Letting Biblical Language Lead Us Beyond Logic

The tensions between God's transcendence and his immanence, between Christ's divinity and his humanity, are not the only paradoxes in Scripture. Other examples of paradoxes in the Bible include God's sovereignty versus humanity's free will and the coexistence of the old nature and the new nature in those who are saved.

I used to come to Scripture with an analytical mindset, and I took great pleasure in playing paradoxical truths against one other. Each time I met a metaphor that pictured one side of a paradox, I would respond to it by saying, "Yes, but . . ." "Yes, God is almighty king, *but* we still have free will." "Yes, Christ's followers are a new creation, *but* the old nature is still strong in us." This kind of response was correct enough from a doctrinal point of view, but I think it diluted the power of the imagery. I was saying to myself, it won't do to take this or that picture in the Bible too seriously; there's another side to the question.

I have come to believe that God does not mean for us to play the two sides of biblical paradoxes against each other, as if each were partly false and needed the other side of the paradox to correct it. Rather, God wants us to experience each side of his paradoxes as fully true and to learn to live in both sides of the truth. That, I think, is one reason God gives us his paradoxical truths not in abstract words that we can balance like careful equations (Christ's humanity versus his divinity, God's sovereignty versus humanity's free will) but in word pictures that have a life of their own and will not be neatly categorized. When we allow powerful images to take hold of us emotionally and imaginatively, they enable us to suspend our compulsive need to make sense of everything. They carry us beyond logic into God's mysterious truths.

In the case of the tension between God's immanence and his transcendence, it is not God's will that we sidestep or dilute either truth. We are to fear and revere him as the mysterious, holy, high and mighty God who dwells in light and speaks in thunder. This side of God was the side we saw in the vision of Christ with a face like the sun and a voice like rushing water in Revelation 1:12-16. And we are to cling to God with childlike confidence because he is the God who reaches down to us with tender concern. This was the side of God we saw in Revelation 1:17, when Jesus soothed John with a gentle touch and reassuring words. The Bible offers us both pictures, but we must be willing to take those pictures seriously and let them impact us.

God has made sure that all the realities we need to know are amply represented in his Word. Often paradoxical truths are held in tension in a single passage. But at other times one pole of a paradox overshadows the other. This is the case in Genesis 2, which gives us a picture of a very human God who labors lovingly over the creation of Adam and makes a false start in solving the "companion problem" before creating Eve. We asked earlier if we should take the imagery of this account seriously. The answer is "Yes!" God surely wants us to revel in his immanence as it is reflected in the anthropomorphisms here: to sense the pleasure he took in forming us, to realize how personally he cares for us and our needs, to rejoice in the many ways we are like him.

Though Genesis 2 catches us up in a picture of God's immanence, we do not have to go far to find a balancing vision of his transcendence. The austere, measured language in the creation account in Genesis 1 portrays a God who simply speaks and brings the worlds into being. There is no experimentation, no hesitation, no physical labor in this story. God is pure, divine mind, vision and voice. This passage and its imagery can bring us to our knees before God's transcendence as surely as the down-to-earth wording of Genesis 2 invites us to celebrate his immanence. God gives us both creation stories because their contrasting images can draw us into a more accurate experience of who he truly is. Our relationship with God would be impoverished if we failed to take the imagery of either passage seriously.

Letting Our Imaginations Find Their Own Way

As we have seen, it's often necessary to try different ways of responding to images in order to find out which way works best for a particular image. Sometimes common sense will tell us whether certain approaches are appropriate. However, there is no universal logic which will show us the "correct" way to read every image we meet in Scripture. Reading literary language is a creative process, a process of individual experimentation as we listen for the way God speaks personally to us through the images he gives us. Since God has made each person unique, it's quite possible for different people to find different yet equally legitimate ways to approach the same passage.

God affirms human creativity in a single surprising verse in Genesis 2.

Now the LORD God had formed out of the ground all the beasts of the field and all the birds of the air. He brought them to the man to see what he would name them; and whatever the man called each living creature, that was its name. (Gen 2:19)

Surely the creator could have named these creatures himself. But instead he invited Adam to join him in the creative process. In a similar way, though God might have communicated to us in some more precise, rigid kind of language, he most often chose to use literary language that gives us room to be creative. In a sense literary passages like the ones we've explored in this chapter invite each of us to "name" them, to put our own personal stamp on them and make them our own.

When I read Genesis 2, I'm aware that my individual background and personality color the way I respond to different parts of this creation story. As one who enjoys ceramic sculpture, I can easily visualize and be inspired by the picture of God molding Adam from clay. However, though the verses about God forming Eve from Adam's rib are equally visual and, in fact, more detailed, I do not find it helpful to picture these verses.

For me, the passage about God removing Adam's rib and creating Eve has a magical quality. If I try to visualize what is happening, I begin by picturing modern surgery with anesthesia, scalpels and stitching. I am transported to a scientific—and for me repulsively gory—realm that is far removed from the atmosphere of wonder I think God wants to communicate through these verses.

Genesis 2:21-23 grabs me with symbolic overtones that appeal to my emotions rather than my senses. I see this passage conveying the mysterious essence of God's gift of maleness and femaleness and his intentions for marriage. The word pictures of a space in Adam's side and a companion formed from his missing rib suggest to me the powerful yet indefinable bond that brought my husband and me together and holds us together. The story captures our deep awareness that we need each other to be complete. When we first discovered we were in love, and when we rediscover periodically the love that sometimes wanes between us, the experience is very like Adam's. It is as if we have been asleep and wake up to find a wonderful surprise, the partner who is just right for us, bone of our bones and flesh of our flesh. We know that the oneness we feel is sheer gift, a creation of God's grace that we could never produce ourselves.

Thus I experience the account of Eve's creation in a realm of symbolic significance that touches me personally though I can't actually visualize the images. However, another person—someone more educated in the wonders of modern medicine and less afraid of it than I am—may visualize surgery when they read this passage and find in that picture a sense of the mystery and miracle that surround God's gift of Eve to Adam. Both responses are legitimate. We have each found a way to hear God speaking personally to us through the images he uses.

Can We Take Some Biblical Imagery Too Seriously?

When we return to the question with which we began this chapter, the answer is a resounding "No!" God has built power into each image he gives us, but that power will be lost on us if we casually dismiss any of the Bible's imagery as too silly or gruesome, too strange or misleading. Trusting God's Word means accepting the possibility that any part of it may have something important to say to us. Our task is to experiment with different ways of reading and to discern which approach best allows a passage to communicate its truths.

We must trust God to give us the insights he wants us to have. On our own we cannot create meanings from biblical language to satisfy our longing to hear God speak, any more than Adam could create for himself a suitable companion to alleviate his loneliness. God put him to sleep, remember, then created Eve and presented her to Adam when he awoke. Similarly we may need to relax a bit before God can speak effectively to us.

Reading the Bible with a kind of mental playfulness, an openness to the unexpected, we can be surprised and delighted when God's words touch and move us. We will not be impatient with ourselves or God when we do not hear him speaking. It is God who makes the connections in our minds, who pours new truths into our hearts. When we read his Word, he invites us to join our creativity with his, but ultimately we must be willing to wait for God to speak to us in his own time and way.

You Are the Body of Christ:

A Bible Study Focused on Imagery of the Human Body

1 Corinthians 12

Please note: In 1 Corinthians 12 Paul deals with the subject of spiritual gifts. In verses 1-11 he emphasizes that there are different kinds of gifts, but they are all given by the same God and they are all given for the common good of the church. In verses 12-27 he supports his points by picturing the church as a body with its different parts.

1. Read 1 Corinthians 12 aloud. Then read verses 12-27 again, from a different version of the Bible.

2. This passage is built around the metaphor of all believers being one in Christ, each being a part of his body (see v. 27). As used by Paul, does the analogy appeal more to your analytical thinking, your senses or your emotions? Explain.

3. Verse 17 presents two strange word pictures. Do you think Paul meant for his readers to visualize these pictures? Why or why not? What effect do they have on you when you visualize them?

4. In verses 15-16, Paul imagines the foot and ear speaking. What tone of voice do you hear them speaking in? How do you think they are feeling?

Have you ever compared yourself to others in your church and thought, "Because I am not _____ , I don't really belong in the church"? (Fill in the blank with the word or words that come to mind.)

5. While verses 15-16 refer to believers who undervalue themselves, verse 21 refers to believers who overvalue themselves and undervalue others. Which type are you more apt to be?

6. Reread 1 Corinthians 12:7-11, 28-30. Here Paul lists some of the spiritual gifts. If you were going to picture these gifts as parts of the body, what part might each gift be?

7. There is a beautiful description of the church as a body in verses 25-26. In all your associations with Christian groups, where have you experienced fellowship that comes closest to the ideal described in these verses?

8. Compare the metaphor of the church as a body used in this chapter with the metaphor of the church as a building used in Ephesians 2:19-22. Which picture speaks more powerfully to you personally? Why?

9. Has this study given you a new vision of your place in the body of Christ? What blessings or gifts has it made you aware of? What challenges might God be calling you to meet?

There is a time for everything,
and a season for every activity under heaven:
a time to be born and a time to die, . . .
a time to weep and a time to laugh,
a time to mourn and a time to dance. (Eccles 3:1-4)

5
Bridging the Historical-Cultural Chasm

We cannot be sure just when the words of Ecclesiastes 3:1-4 were written or who wrote them, but we don't need to know the historical context in order to relate to this passage. It grapples with a question people have always asked: How can I make sense of life's unpredictable ups and downs, its surprising joy and pain? Over the centuries the essential ingredients—comic and tragic—of the human drama have remained the same. Thus these poignant words from Ecclesiastes, written over 2,000 years ago by a sage somewhere in the Near East, could serve as lyrics for a song that was popular in the United States during the Vietnam War.[1]

Our focus on animal imagery, water imagery and body imagery in the preceding chapters has shown that most of the word pictures in the Bible, when read in context, have an elemental power to evoke the appropriate response in us. In this chapter we will find that most of the human drama in Scripture has the same kind of universal appeal that can move our emotions and spirits. Too often, at least for purposes of a literary reading of the Bible, we make the mistake of exaggerating the cultural gap that exists between the writers of the Bible and modern readers. We stumble over the strange elements in Scripture and fail to notice how many of its stories and pictures reflect what we face and what we feel today.

The story of Abraham and Sarah is a good case in point. When we first meet Abraham and his family in the pages of Genesis, they seem far removed from our experience, living in tents and roaming the desert 4,000 years ago. We wonder if there is any way we can relate to them. But as soon as we realize that Abraham and Sarah were a childless couple longing for a baby, we can begin to get caught up in their story. We can share their exuberant joy when Isaac is finally born. And later, when God gives his shocking command for Abraham to sacrifice Isaac, we can imagine the pain and terror this father of long ago must have experienced as he contemplated his precious child's death.

This chapter will focus on the contrasting dramas of birth and death as they are played out in Bible narratives and suggested in biblical imagery. Surely no human experiences are more elemental or more emotional. Looking at stories involving birth and death will show us how easily we can relate to the drama that is such a large part of the Bible's literary power.

Stories of Birth Pack Universal Power

Certain dramatic sequences never fail to bring a lump to my throat, though I have seen them scores of times in movies and on television. Among these predictably moving scenes are the husband's happy reaction when his wife tells him they are expecting a baby and the infant's lusty cry announcing a safe arrival. These are powerful images because they capture the emotional experience of birth.

Conflicting feelings surround birth. Anxious waiting is one of them, for birth is fraught with uncertainty. Will the child be a boy or girl, healthy or sickly, a source of pleasure or a source of pain? However, birth is associated with hopeful expectancy as well. Who knows what difference this tiny new person may make, what ends he may achieve, what dreams she may fulfill?

Birth also brings a sense of helplessness and humility. From the moment of conception through the months of waiting to the time of delivery, the coming of new life is mysterious and out of our control. A baby is a gift, springing from our bodies and yet not really ours. In awe we witness a miracle, creation reenacted as a new little person enters the world. And yet we have been a vital part of that miracle; the baby is in some sense our creation. Our humility is mingled with unabashed pride.

When a birth goes well, joy and relief are accompanied by a frightening sense of responsibility. A long wait and a painful ordeal are over, but the hardest part lies ahead. This fragile life must be nurtured, and faith and courage will be called for.

Birth has always evoked these feelings of anxiety, hope, helplessness, awe, pride, joy, devotion and faith. Naturally we find these same emotions energizing the accounts of birth in the Bible, from Isaac to Jesus.

These stories are historical, but they are also highly dramatic and essentially literary. Too many of us left school with the impression that history is distant, dry and dull. We are apt to read the historical sections of the Bible expecting them to be this way. But Bible history is salvation history. God wants it to capture our emotions as well as inform our minds, so he presents this history in the form of vivid, riveting stories.

Birth's Crucial Role in Salvation History

Have you ever noticed the large part birth stories play in salvation history? God's plan of salvation in the Bible begins to unfold when he calls Abraham out of his country into the land of Canaan. God promises that Abraham's descendants will be a great nation and bring blessing to the whole world. Yet the fulfillment of this mighty promise is bundled up in one pivotal event: Abraham and Sarah must have a baby of their own.

Anyone who has hoped big hopes and dreamed big dreams for a baby-on-the-way can identify with the intense expectancy Abraham and Sarah feel when God promises them this special child. But we can also feel with them their mounting anxiety as time passes. After all, they are already very old when God promises them offspring. How will he keep his promise? They hope for a miracle, but as Sarah fails to conceive year after year, we hear their growing disappointment in Abraham's plaintive words: "O Sovereign LORD, what can you give me since I remain childless? . . . A servant in my household will be my heir" (Gen 15:2-3).

Abraham and Sarah are helpless to make God's promise come true. We can understand why they try to take control of the situation themselves, agreeing that Abraham will sleep with Sarah's maidservant Hagar, hoping to build a family through her. But their efforts only result in strife and disappointment, for Hagar's son, Ishmael, is not the child God intends to use to carry forward his purposes (see Gen 16; 17:18-22).

Each time God repeats his promise, we sense that it is becoming harder and harder for Abraham and Sarah to believe. When God assures the ninety-nine-year-old Abraham that Sarah will be "the mother of nations," he laughs incredulously and pleads with God to let Ishmael be his heir (Gen 17:17-18). Sarah laughs too when she overhears the Lord tell her husband, "I will surely return to you about this time next year, and Sarah your wife will have a son" (Gen 18:10). Yet they cling to faith, even in the midst of their doubts. What else can they do? God is in control.

Finally Isaac is born. In Sarah's words we catch the elation and sense of wonder that accompany the birth.

"God has brought me laughter, and everyone who hears about this will laugh with me." And she added, "Who would have said to Abraham that Sarah would nurse children? Yet I have borne him a son in his old age." (Gen 21:6-7)

Sarah's and Abraham's feelings of hope and disappointment, anxiety and faith, humility and elation draw us into the opening act of God's great drama of salvation.

When we reach the climactic act in that drama, the long-awaited coming of the Messiah, the Bible gives us not one birth story but two stories intertwined—the birth of John the Baptist and the birth of Jesus. Angels appear to Zechariah, Mary and Joseph to tell them about God's special plans for the babies that are coming. The long-barren Elizabeth and the young virgin Mary share their joy as expectant mothers. Miraculous happenings mingle with humble human concerns in the nativity accounts. The triumphant jubilation of the angelic chorus contrasts with Herod's murderous jealousy as the Christ child is born. Here is all the drama, pathos, suspense, conflict and spectacle we could want in a story. It is as if God pulled out all the stops, exploiting all the emotive power that is associated with birth, when he planned his Son's entrance into human history.

We must marvel at God's graciousness, that he should choose to carry his great plan of salvation forward through the simple and appealing drama of human birth. God could have mapped out some esoteric redemptive strategy by which his human creatures would struggle to ascend to heaven. But he chose instead to stoop to our level, to come to us on terms we could all under-stand. He channeled his salvation through the birth of babies, one generation after another, until God himself became a baby in the person of Jesus. The birth stories in Scripture are potent evidence of the way God reaches into the world to bring his sinful creatures new life. If we open ourselves to the language of these stories, they can capture our hearts and carry us toward a new birth of our own.

A Birth Ritual We Cannot Relate To

To get personally involved in the birth stories of Scripture, we simply need to exercise our imaginations, asking, for example: What must Mary and Joseph have been thinking and feeling? How would I have felt in their situation? However, we cannot relate so immediately to all the human attitudes and behavior we encounter in God's Word, for a historical-cultural gap—in fact, a chasm—does separate contemporary Americans from the world of the Bible. Not only are we at least twenty to thirty centuries removed from the time the Scriptures were written; we also live in the West, while the biblical texts grew out of an Eastern milieu.

The differences in perspective become evident when we come to biblical references to circumcision, the ritual most closely tied to childbirth in the Bible. It is not that we no longer practice circumcision. Many boys born in this country are circumcised shortly after birth as a routine medical procedure. But circum-cision was obviously something more than a routine medical procedure in the Bible, as the following verses indicate.

The LORD your God will circumcise your hearts and the hearts of your descendants, so that you may love him with all your heart and with all your soul, and live. (Deut 30:6)

To whom can I address myself,
to whom give solemn warning? Who will hear me?
Their ears are uncircumcised;
they cannot listen;
they treat the LORD's word as a reproach;
they show no concern with it. (Jer 6:10, NEB)

We stumble over verses like these which use circumcision metaphorically. They do not speak to anything in our own experience. Before we can relate to them, we must find a way to get back into the world out of which the images grew.

We can learn the origin and significance of circumcision by reading Genesis 17. There we learn that God had instituted the ritual with Abraham before Isaac was born, telling him that he and all his male descendants must be circumcised as a sign that they belonged to God's chosen people. All Jews through the centuries were to signify their commitment to this special covenant relationship with God by performing the rite of circumcision on their male babies. It was to remain a "sign in the flesh" of God's special grace to them and their response to that grace.

It is hard to think of any visible symbols we use today which are comparable. Perhaps we might visualize God giving the rite of circumcision to Abraham and his descendants as a groom gives a ring to his bride, sealing their commitment to each other. The Jews repeated the rite with each boy just as a wife keeps the ring constantly on her finger, symbolizing that her love for her husband remains unchanged.

Yet circumcision, like other important symbolic actions, sometimes lost its meaning for the people who performed it. As the passages quoted earlier indicate, God's people often went through the motions of the rite without any real commitment to their God, just as people today may wear their wedding rings when their hearts are not in the relationship. God had to remind the Israelites that it was not a superficial ceremony he wanted, but "circumcised ears" that would listen to him and "circumcised hearts" that would respond to him in love and obedience.

Circumcision is referred to more often in the New Testament than in the Old. Paul in particular seems to focus often on circumcision, presenting it in both a positive and a negative light. Clearly he believes that his circumcision metaphors will carry great power, but they may only confuse modern readers unless we fill in some historical background. A Bible dictionary can help us understand the Jewish attitude toward circumcision that had developed by the time of the first century when Paul was writing.

Since circumcision was a religious ritual celebrated in the family circle, not in the temple in Jerusalem, it became more important to the Jews during their exile in Babylon. After the Jews returned to their land, they continued to be under foreign domination. When the Greeks and, later, the Romans occupied Palestine, the Jews clung to circumcision as a sign of their special national identity as God's chosen people. Sometimes they were persecuted, even killed for this practice, which was considered barbaric and indecent by the Greeks and Romans.

By the time of Christ, the Jews had largely forgotten that God had chosen them, blessed them and established a special relationship with them so that they could be a blessing to all peoples on earth. Under foreign rule their frustration and bitterness against Gentiles had mounted. They hated being underdogs, and they soothed their wounded pride by reassuring themselves that—

since they were God's chosen people who kept God's laws—they were far superior to their conquerors. The strict Jews practiced careful segregation from the foreigners so they would not be contaminated by them. Meanwhile they looked forward to the day when Abraham's children, "the circumcision," would be part of the coming kingdom of God that Messiah would bring, a kingdom of which the uncircumcised Gentiles would have no part.

Circumcision had become for first-century Jews not a symbol of God's grace to them and their response to that grace, but a badge of their supposed righteousness, their superiority to other people in the eyes of God.[2] Many of the Jews who became Christians carried this attitude into the early church and insisted that gentile converts must follow the Jewish law and be circumcised. Paul denounced these Judaizers, condemning them for continuing to "put confidence in the flesh," continuing to believe that they somehow earned God's favor by following the law.

Paul knew Christ had established a new covenant. Like the old covenant, it was essentially a covenant of grace that made possible a special relationship with God. But now God had made it clear that that relationship depended only on faith, not on success in keeping the law; moreover, it was open to all peoples, not just the Jews. Paul had been called by God specifically to bring this good news to the Gentiles:

> *You who are Gentiles by birth and called "uncircumcised" by those who call themselves "the circumcision". . . now in Christ Jesus you who once were far away have been brought near through the blood of Christ. (Eph 2:11, 13)*

> *In him you were also circumcised, in the putting off of the sinful nature,*

not with a circumcision done by the hands of men but with the circumcision done by Christ. . . . When you were dead in your sins and in the uncir-cumcision of your sinful nature, God made you alive with Christ. (Col 2:11, 13)

There was no room in this new covenant for pride or boasting. A person's salvation depended on Christ's sacrifice alone, not on whether he or she kept God's law. Because Paul could see that the attitudes of those who insisted on circumcision threatened to undercut the very foundation of the gospel, he used graphic language to warn people of the danger.

Watch out for those dogs, those men who do evil, those mutilators of the flesh. For it is we who are the circumcision, we who worship by the Spirit of God, who glory in Christ Jesus, and who put no confidence in the flesh. (Phil 3:2-3)

May I never boast except in the cross of our Lord Jesus Christ. . . . Neither circumcision nor uncircumcision means anything; what counts is a new creation. (Gal 6:14-15)

We cannot expect to respond spontaneously to the circumcision imagery in these verses the way we can to the birth stories in the Bible. However, once we gain the necessary historical back-ground from the Old Testament and from reference books, cir-cumcision language can speak to us powerfully about God's grace, the wholehearted response he expects from us, and our tendency to fall into the trap of legalism and self-righteousness.

Death Narratives Move Us Toward God
Stories of death can move us as powerfully as stories of birth,

though of course our emotions will be different. When we read a simple newspaper account of the sudden death of a stranger whose age is close to that of a spouse or child, we can almost feel a cold hand squeezing our heart. When the television screen flashes pictures of plane wreckage and bodies strewn over a crash site, the truth of our mortality comes crashing in on us.

The Bible contains many poignant and chilling accounts of death. Moses dies on Mount Nebo, in sight of the Promised Land yet prevented by God from entering into it (Deut 34:1-8). Saul falls on his own sword before enemy soldiers can kill him (1 Sam 31:1-7). Ananias and Sapphira drop dead when they lie to their brothers in the early church (Acts 4:32—5:10).

These stories have the power to frighten and repel us. God wants us to respond this way. Human death is usually presented in the Bible as a curse, God's penalty for sin.[3] Note God's accusing words to Moses just before his death:

"There on the mountain that you have climbed you will die and be gathered to your people, just as your brother Aaron died on Mount Hor and was gathered to his people. This is because both of you broke faith with me in the presence of the Israelites . . . and because you did not uphold my holiness among the Israelites. Therefore, you will see the land only from a distance; you will not enter the land I am giving to the people of Israel." (Deut 32:50-52)

We can imagine Moses' feelings as he hears these words. Death will prevent him from reaching the goal he has pursued for forty years. Our hearts hurt for him.

The stories of death in God's Word set before us a choice, the same choice Moses set before the Israelites at the end of his life.

I set before you today life and prosperity, death and destruction. For I command you today to love the LORD your God, to walk in his ways, and to keep his commands, decrees and laws; then you will live and increase.

. . . But if your heart turns away and you are not obedient, . . . you will certainly be destroyed. . . . I have set before you life and death, blessings and curses. Now choose life, so that you and your children may live and that you may love the LORD your God, listen to his voice, and hold fast to him. For the LORD is your life. (Deut 30:15-20)

Since many of the death accounts in Scripture evoke our natural feelings of fear, grief and revulsion, they operate somewhat like "hellfire and damnation" preaching. When we open ourselves to their repulsive power, they give us a forceful emotional nudge to choose God and the real life he offers. Thus these accounts demonstrate God's gracious desire to save us as surely as do the birth stories in the Bible.

Death Rituals Outside Our Experience

Although the basic drama of death is something all human beings experience, there is much biblical imagery, based on the rituals that accompanied death, which is foreign to us today. We meet such imagery in the opening scenes of the book of Job.

Another messenger came and said [to Job], "Your sons and daughters were feasting and drinking wine at the oldest brother's house, when suddenly a mighty wind swept in from the desert and struck the four corners of the house. It collapsed on them and they are dead, and I am the only one who has escaped to tell you!"

At this, Job got up and tore his robe and shaved his head. Then he fell to the ground in worship and said:

"Naked I came from my mother's womb,
and naked I will depart.
The LORD gave and the LORD has taken away;
may the name of the LORD be praised." (Job 1:18-21)

When Job's three friends . . . heard about all the troubles that had come upon him, they set out from their homes and met together by agreement to go and sympathize with him and comfort him. When they saw him from a distance, . . . they began to weep aloud, and they tore their robes and sprinkled dust on their heads. Then they sat on the ground with him for seven days and seven nights. (Job 2:11-13)

We may be puzzled by the behavior of Job and his friends. Surely he must have loved his children very much, but he has a funny way of showing it. And presumably his friends came to comfort him, but their actions too seem odd.

To relate to the account of Job and his friends, and to many other such passages in the Bible, it is helpful to acquaint ourselves with ancient Near-Eastern mourning rituals. Reference books on biblical culture will tell us what usually happened when someone died in Bible times.

In the ancient Near East, death was never glossed over or hushed up. Custom provided ways for people to express their grief openly, noisily, even violently. When people heard of a death, they tore their garments. People would cry, moan, beat their breasts and cover their heads with their hands. Some would don old dirty clothes or even sackcloth, a coarse material worn around the waist next to the skin. Sometimes they threw soil over their heads, rolled in the dust or sat among ashes. They fasted, and some shaved their hair or even cut their bodies.

Burial usually took place on the day of death. The funeral procession was public and noisy. Flutists might be hired for the occasion, as well as professional mourners, usually women. They sang or cried loud laments as they accompanied the corpse to the place of burial. Not only family and close friends came to a funeral. Anyone who heard of or saw a funeral procession was obliged to join it and participate in the noisy grieving.

Ritual mourning would continue for seven days after the funeral. Visiting and comforting the bereaved was very important during this time. Friends and neighbors brought food and drink to the house of death, since it was ritually unclean and food could not be prepared there. During this period, mourners sat barefoot on the ground. They were forbidden to work, wash, anoint themselves, engage in sex or study the Torah.

These mourning customs were a socially acceptable expression of deeply felt pain and grief. Armed with a knowledge of these customs, we can approach the account in Job with more understanding. We can see that he was truly grieved by his children's death, as he demonstrated by tearing his garments and shaving his head. His friends were true comforters. By weeping loudly, tearing their clothes, sprinkling dust on their heads and sitting on the ground with Job for days, they were participating in his grief in the usual way prescribed by their culture.

Consider also this passionate passage in Micah, which shows God mourning over his idolatrous people whom he must punish. The following are God's words:

I will make Samaria a heap of rubble. . . .
All her idols will be broken to pieces;
*   all her temple gifts will be burned with fire;*
*   I will destroy all her images. . . .*
Because of this I will weep and wail;
*   I will go about barefoot and naked.*
I will howl like a jackal
*   and moan like an owl.*
For her wound is incurable;
*   it has come to Judah.*
It has reached the very gate of my people,

even to Jerusalem itself. (Mic 1:6-9)

Without knowing about the mourning customs of going barefoot, lamenting loudly, and wearing sackcloth (the nakedness referred to in this context probably indicates the wearing of a rudimentary sackcloth garment, something like a loincloth),[4] we could not appreciate the pathos of this passage nor the love of God for his people that it expresses. Instead we might easily be offended by the picture of God barefoot and naked, howling and moaning like an animal.

Bridging the Gap

Clearly, learning the historical-cultural background of Bible passages is often helpful and sometimes essential. There are good reference books that go beyond stating dry facts to convey a feel for the times and the personality of the people.[5] Historical novels too may help us transport ourselves into the biblical world. But we will be surprised how often simply tuning in to our own feelings and experiences can enable us to bridge the gap between ourselves and the people of the Bible.

As we think again of the story of Abraham and Sarah, we can see a way in which our "advanced culture" has in a sense come full circle and brought us closer to these ancient people. Currently our society is particularly sensitive to the pain which infertility brings. More and more couples are finding they cannot conceive. Technology has opened up options that Abraham and Sarah could never have imagined, and couples are willing to go to great lengths (including hiring surrogate mothers) in order to have a child who belongs biologically to at least one parent. Under the circumstances, we find that Abraham's plan to produce an heir through Hagar does not sound particularly foreign to us.

Sometimes trends in our culture do make it difficult to identify with the attitudes and behavior portrayed in the Bible. It's questionable whether most of us can feel the wrenching horror of death with quite the intensity felt by people in Bible times; we no longer have vivid customs that allow us to express that horror. In many ways our culture has swept death under the rug. Wearing black at funerals is out of fashion. People usually die now out of sight in a hospital, and their corpses are kept hidden in closed caskets. I suspect our society tries to play down death because death challenges our delusion that our technology gives us control of our lives.

Yet we all experience the death of those we love, and with a little effort we can empathize with—perhaps even envy—the dramatic ways the people of the Bible reacted to death, just as we can relate to their feelings about birth. Resource books may help us get back into the world of the Bible, but we should not substitute these books for our own imaginative involvement in the text. Only when we personally identify with the people we read about and enter into their weeping and laughing, their mourning and dancing, will God speak directly to us through their stories. By opening our emotions to the human drama in Scripture, we open ourselves to God.

Death Overtakes the Uncircumcised in Heart:

A Bible Study Focused on Imagery Related to Birth and Death

Jeremiah 9:3-26

Please note: Before reading the passage for this study, reread the sections from chapter two that provide historical background to the book of Jeremiah.

1. In Jeremiah 9:3-26 we hear words God speaks to the people of Judah through his prophet Jeremiah. Read this passage aloud from two versions of the Bible. As you listen to the words, what tone (or tones) of voice do you hear God using? Jot down your impressions.

2. In this passage, God says he has no other choice than to punish his people for the sins they have committed (vv. 7-9). What sins does he accuse them of (see especially vv. 3-8, 13-14)? Do you think his accusations apply equally well to our contemporary American society? Why or why not?

3. In verses 10-22, God gives several graphic descriptions (some literal, some figurative) of the punishment he will bring on the nation of Judah. If you had been in Jeremiah's audience, which description would have disturbed you most? Why?

4. How would most Americans react if someone told us God was going to punish our nation because of the sins we have committed?

Please note: This Jeremiah passage does refer to certain ancient Near-Eastern funeral customs which are not familiar to us. Verses 10 and 20 refer to laments (other versions call them dirges or funeral songs), and in verse 17 God says it is time to call for the women who are professional mourners. Each of these references precedes a description not of something that will happen but of something that has already happened. (See vv. 10, 18-19, 21.) Thus these funeral images, which would have been readily understood by Jeremiah's audience, were used to make his listeners feel as if God's punishment had already come and they were observers at their own funeral.

5. What if God allowed you to see a vision of your own funeral following an unexpected and terrible death? What would be the impact of that vision on you? What might it cause you to do?

6. Review the historical background on circumcision given in this chapter. How do you think Jeremiah's audience reacted to the words of verses 25-26?

7. What does the phrase "uncircumcised in heart" mean to you? How might a Christian today who is "uncircumcised in heart" act?

8. In some versions of the Bible, verse 10 is presented as if Jeremiah is mourning over Judah's ruin. But in other versions (NASB, NEB, KJV), God himself is shown weeping and wailing over his ruined nation. Do you ever picture God weeping over sinners and the suffering they bring on themselves? Do you think God wants us to see him this way? Explain your answer.

9. As you have read this passage imaginatively, have you become aware that there is some corner of your heart that is "uncircumcised"? Is there some part of your life that you are withholding from God? Write a lament as if God is weeping over the deadness and desolation of that uncircumcised part of your life.

Look, the Lamb of God, who takes away the sin of the world!
(Jn 1:29)

God was pleased to have all his fullness dwell in him, and
through him to reconcile to himself all things, whether things
on earth or things in heaven, by making peace through his
blood, shed on the cross. (Col 1:19-20)

6
Rediscovering the Drama Behind Doctrine

*T*he first five chapters of this book touched on a variety of images with many diverse meanings. Those chapters taught how to apply basic principles of reading that enable us to respond personally when God speaks to us in literary language. This chapter and the following one take a different approach, exploring in depth two of the central motifs in Scripture—atoning sacrifice and courtroom confrontation. The purpose of these chapters is to show more profoundly the surprising power of the principles taught in chapters 1-5.

Look at the picture painted in John 1:29. How can a lamb—helpless and innocent—take away the sin of the world? Listen to the drama in Colossians 1:19-20. How can one man—dying slowly, horribly on a cross—reconcile everything to God? The startling language in these verses evokes that single, shocking event on Calvary around which human history revolves. Yet if we're asked to explain this language, we're apt to answer mechanically, "It teaches the doctrine of the atonement: Jesus died for our sins so that we might be reconciled to God."

We have a tendency to reduce much of Scripture to doctrine. Of course it is legitimate to define biblical doctrines. Doctrines are like the bones of our faith. Just as studying a skeleton in an anatomy class helps us understand how the human body is put together, tracing doctrines in Scripture helps us see the theological patterns that make God's Word hang together. But doctrines alone are like bones without flesh and blood on them. They are abstractions without the imagery and drama that enable us to experience truth more personally.

Perhaps we have the idea that doctrines are the real meat of biblical truth. We may suspect that babies in the faith can only take in picture language, such as "being washed in the blood of the lamb," but we assume that more sophisticated believers will be nourished by theological concepts such as "the atonement." However, if we read the Bible with this mindset, we are cheating ourselves. Too much emphasis on doctrine may actually short-circuit God's desire to touch us directly through his Word. Scripture's real power resides in the dramas that lie behind the doctrines of our faith.

In this chapter we will view Christ's atoning death as drama—heart-rending, mind-wrenching drama. In fact, we will discover that his dying was the climax of two historical dramas. The first drama unfolded during the brief years of Jesus' earthly ministry, as a volatile mix of social, political and religious forces in Palestine combined to oppose Jesus and finally execute him. The second drama unfolded over many centuries as the people of Israel performed their traditional temple sacrifices until God sent his Son as the sacrifice to end all sacrifices.

Seeing Drama in the Events Leading to Jesus' Death

In the first chain of events that contributes to the atonement drama, we watch an itinerant rabbi, Jesus of Nazareth, getting "caught between the forces of power politics."[1] The Jewish elite bring him to trial and Roman authorities hang him on a cross as a common criminal. The narrative of the days and hours preceding his death is the most intensely dramatic story in all the Bible. If we read through all four Gospel accounts of the week of Jesus' execution (accounts which reinforce one another by giving a somewhat different slant on the same events), we find ourselves emotionally drawn into the drama.

It is a drama that we must view as a tragedy. Jesus' death, which Jesus has been alluding to for months, becomes ghastly reality as his cruelly scourged body hangs nailed to the cross. Added to the sheer horror of this gruesome mode of execution is our shock at seeing how callously the religious leaders of Israel deal with Jesus. Their rigged trial of this innocent man affronts our sense of justice. We cry out against the ruthless way Jesus' enemies corner him, condemn him and crucify him.

Perhaps more poignant even than the unjust treatment by his enemies is the way Jesus' friends betray him. First Judas, one of the twelve Jesus has specially chosen and loved, goes to the high priest and sells out his master for thirty pieces of silver. Shortly we see Jesus' other disciples deserting him too, both emotionally and physically.

We know that all through the Last Supper Jesus is intensely aware of the ordeal he must face. These final hours with his friends are precious to him. "I have eagerly desired to eat this Passover with you before I suffer," he tells them, and goes on to explain that one of them will betray him and that he will die. Imagine how he feels when they begin arguing among themselves over which of them is the greatest (see Luke's account in Lk 22:21-24). In its own way their callousness rivals that of the Jewish leaders who will try Jesus. Later, in Gethsemane, he asks his closest friends, Peter, James and John, for their help. "My soul is overwhelmed with sorrow to the point of death. Stay here and keep watch with me." When he returns to find them sleeping, his sharp disappointment comes through in his words: "Could you men not keep watch with me for one hour?" (see Mt 26:36-46). When Jesus is arrested, all his disciples flee to save their own skins. A short time later Jesus witnesses Peter's betrayal (Lk 22:61) as he denies three times even knowing the Master. Then during the trial before Pilate, the crowds—who only days before had acclaimed him with palm branches and shouts of hosanna—now shout, "Crucify him! Crucify him!"

Finally on the cross Christ experiences abandonment by God himself. As he takes the full weight of our sins upon himself, he suffers the separation from his Father that such sin deserves. His loud cry shocks us. "My God, my God, why have you forsaken me?" (Mt 27:46; Mk 15:34).

Death, injustice, betrayal and desertion—all these elements catch us up in a profound sense of tragedy when we read the Passion narratives in the Gospels. Nevertheless, if we read these accounts all the way through we sense that tragedy is not the only mood, or even the dominant mood, in these narratives. Jesus should seem like the victim of a cruel fate in this drama, but he does not come across as a victim.

Jesus cannot be seen as a victim because he foresees so clearly and accepts so completely the things he will suffer. He predicts Judas' betrayal, Peter's triple denial, the fact that his disciples will scatter when he is arrested. Nothing takes him by surprise.

But more than this, we have the sense that Jesus and his Father are orchestrating—we might even say staging—all the events of the final week before his execution. We watch these events unfolding like a pageant. The atmosphere is one of a solemn celebration that builds toward a profoundly significant climax. With regal dignity Jesus holds center stage as he leads the ritual procession toward his own death.

The procession begins with Jesus' triumphal entry into Jerusalem. Jesus sends his disciples to borrow a colt so he can enter the Holy City as prophesied in Zechariah, and he clearly intends that people will greet him as the expected Messiah king, spreading cloaks and branches on the road before him and shouting praises. When the Jewish leaders tell Jesus he should rebuke his followers, he replies, "I tell you, . . . if they keep quiet, the stones will cry out" (Lk 19:40). Jesus sees his death approaching, yet he sees it as perfectly appropriate that people should greet this event with rejoicing. In the midst of the throng's elation he weeps, not because he must die but because the people are cheering him for the wrong reasons. He knows that when he dies for their salvation, many will reject the salvation he brings. In the days following the triumphal entry, as Jesus teaches in the temple, his parables repeatedly point toward his death and beyond it to his return.

Another element of ritual is introduced when Jesus is at a dinner with friends and Mary anoints him with expensive perfume.[2] Mary probably performs the anointing as a tribute to her Lord, but Jesus reads a deeper meaning into her action. She poured perfume on him, he says, to prepare him for his burial, a gesture so perfect that it will be recalled whenever the gospel is preached. Here again we see Jesus' awareness that his impending death will be good news for the whole world. It is only appropriate that such a beautiful ceremony should precede a seemingly ugly execution.

Of course Jesus' Last Supper with his disciples has a powerful ritual quality, for they are celebrating the greatest Jewish feast. However, Jesus makes the ceremony not one that looks back to Israel's escape from Egypt, but one that looks forward to his own death. Jesus tells his disciples, "I will not eat [this Passover] again until it finds fulfillment in the kingdom of God. . . . This is my body given for you. . . . This cup is the new covenant in my blood, which is poured out for you" (Lk 22:16-20). Even though Jesus' words speak of suffering and death, they point to the good news of a new covenant and the coming kingdom. John's Gospel describes Jesus' last evening with his disciples differently, yet the atmosphere is still highly ceremonial, beginning with foot washing and ending with Jesus' solemn prayers for himself, his disciples and all believers to come.

The sense of ceremony that follows Jesus as he moves toward his death continues in his arrest. With great dignity Jesus goes to meet his enemies and surrenders himself to them. John reports that the soldiers who come to arrest him fall at his feet (Jn 18:6). Later the Roman soldiers, in their efforts to humiliate him, actually affirm his kingship when they put a scarlet robe on him, place a crown of thorns on his head, and kneel before him saying, "Hail, King of the Jews!" It is as if everyone, either wittingly or unwittingly, must perform their preordained roles in the pageant of salvation God has planned.

The procession Jesus has been leading ends at the cross, and there the drama reaches its conclusion. As Jesus hangs dying, the sun stops shining and darkness falls over the land. Then Jesus cries out, "It is finished!" The earth shakes, rocks split and graves open. These "special effects" underline just how momentous this solemn ceremony of death has been. One of the Romans who killed Jesus is compelled by this grand finale to exclaim, "Surely he was the Son of God" (Mt 27:54).

Jesus' Death and Old Testament Sacrifice

As readers of the Gospels' Passion stories, we can sense the triumphant ceremonial tone of Jesus' progress toward the cross. But we may not grasp the full significance of that ceremonial tone. Jesus' disciples sensed the triumphant atmosphere in many of the events that preceded his death, but they failed to grasp just what kind of ceremony they were witnessing. They assumed his triumph would be an earthly victory, a political victory. Expecting that their master would establish his kingdom in power, they consistently misunderstood and dismissed his declarations that he must die. When arrest and trial, torture and execution came for Jesus, his disciples' dreams died too. In the dark hours following the crucifixion, they could not view his death as anything but tragic.

How did the disciples come to see that Jesus' death was something to celebrate, the greatest news of all time? Of course Christ's resurrection had much to do with changing their despair into confident joy. In the book of Acts the resurrection is the chief evidence Jesus' followers set forth to prove that he is the Messiah who can save the world from sin. But elsewhere, in the Epistles and Revelation, the writers emphasize more strongly that Jesus' triumph was evidenced not only in his resurrection but in his death itself.

This positive perspective on the cross was possible because Jesus' followers realized his death was not just the climax of a power struggle in first-century Palestine. It was the climax of another historical chain of events as well. The disciples, like

Unlocking the Power of God's Word

their ancestors for generations, had gone to the temple regularly to participate in the blood sacrifices of their faith. Now they came to understand that Jesus' death, which looked to all the world like a political execution, was in truth the culmination of their sacrificial system, the ultimate atoning sacrifice.[3]

All through the language of the New Testament we find Jesus' crucifixion described in terms that belong to the drama of temple sacrifice. This language helped the early Christians experience the cross of Christ as good news. When they remembered their Lord hanging on the cross, they could also visualize him as the Passover lamb being slaughtered at the altar. When they recalled blood flowing from his pierced side, they could also see forgiveness flowing out to cover their sins. Though they cringed at the memory of his scourged body succumbing to death, they could perceive behind this shameful miscarriage of justice a sacrifice that reconciled a fallen world to God.

The tragedy of execution was wrapped up with the pageant of religious ritual in the minds of the early Christians, in order to help them grasp the saving power of Jesus' death; we must ourselves enter imaginatively into both aspects of this drama if it is to have power for us. But while we can feel, along with the early believers, the horror of Jesus' unjust execution, it is much harder for us to relate to the wonder of his sacrifice. Images of innocent animals being slaughtered and blood being splashed against the altar strike us as repulsive and primitive. It's no wonder we are more comfortable seeing the atonement as dry doctrine than entering into its essential drama. Yet unless we can feel what sacrifice meant to the Jewish people, we will not be able to feel the full force of what Jesus did for us on the cross.

Old Testament Sacrifice: God's Gracious Gift

We are apt to think of sacrifices as gifts offered by superstitious people to placate or manipulate the gods. But Old Testament laws concerning sacrifice make it clear that atoning sacrifice was a wonderful gift given by God to his people. As God explained to Moses, "The life of a creature is in the blood, and I have given it to you to make atonement for yourselves on the altar" (Lev 17:11).

God had revealed himself to the Israelites as a Holy God who must, by his very nature, be angry at sin and punish it. But Yahweh mercifully provided a way for his people to avert his wrath if they carefully obeyed his commands. They must bring an animal without any defect to his house and kill it there. Priests whom God had appointed to be mediators between himself and his people would approach the altar to sprinkle the animal's blood and burn all or part of the fat and flesh. God assured the people that such an offering would please him, would turn aside his anger and re-establish a right relationship between themselves and their Holy God.

For the Israelites, sacrifice was a profoundly moving experience, part solemn ritual, part joyous celebration. As a worshiping community they gathered in the impressive setting of the temple. There they witnessed the dramatic pageantry of colorful priestly garments and red spurting blood. They heard trumpets blaring and animals bellowing and bleating. As they laid their hands on the head of each victim, they felt the warmth and energy of each animal before they took its life. They smelled the pungent odor of burning flesh and incense as the smoke rose from the altar. Finally they tasted the fellowship meal. God designed the ritual so that his people could experience with all their senses both the life-and-death seriousness of their own sin and the amazing generosity of his forgiveness.

For centuries God's chosen people claimed his mercy through the sacrifices they performed. However, they did not understand that these rites were leading up to a far greater sacrifice. The Old Testament ceremonies were only a partial, blurred picture of how God intended to save all people from sin forever. When Jesus was crucified, that picture came into focus. God had sent his Son, the Messiah, to be the perfect sacrifice for the atonement of the sins of the world.

God purposely timed the crucifixion so that it would be seen as an atoning sacrifice. It was no accident that Jesus should come to Jerusalem to die at Passover. It was God's perfect plan.[4] Passover was the festival when Jews from all over the world came to their Holy City to sacrifice lambs in the temple and eat them to commemorate the freeing of the Israelites from bondage in Egypt.

When Jesus ate his last Passover meal with his disciples, he explained that his death would be an atoning sacrifice for sin.

While they were eating, Jesus took bread, gave thanks and broke it, and gave it to his disciples, saying, "Take and eat; this is my body."

Then he took the cup, gave thanks and offered it to them, saying, "Drink from it, all of you. This is my blood of the covenant, which is poured out for many for the forgiveness of sins." (Mt 26:26-28)

The disciples did not understand then the significance of Jesus' words. It was only later that they realized Jesus was to be seen as the sacrificial lamb whose broken body and spilled blood released people from their bondage to sin and brought them into new freedom and fellowship with God.

Much of the language attached to the crucifixion in the Epistles intentionally calls up the picture of Jesus as atoning sacrifice. Paul declares explicitly, "Christ, our Passover lamb, has been sacrificed" (1 Cor 5:7). Central to the picture in Romans of how God has justified sinners is Paul's insistence that Jesus' death was "a sacrifice of atonement" (Rom 3:25), "a sin offering" (Rom 8:3).

Peter too emphasizes the sacrificial nature of Jesus' death.

Christ suffered for you. . . .

> *"He committed no sin,*
> *and no deceit was found in his mouth."*

He himself bore our sins in his body on the tree, so that we might die to sins and live for righteousness; by his wounds you have been healed. For you were like sheep going astray, but now you have returned to the Shepherd and Overseer of your souls. (1 Pet 2:21-22, 24-25)

Here Peter obviously views his Lord as fulfilling the purpose of Old Testament sacrifice: he is the victim without blemish who bears people's sins so that they may be reconciled to God.

Because those who preached the gospel message used language which echoed the Old Testament regulations concerning sacrifice, their Jewish listeners could begin to grasp what Christ's death had done for them; Gentiles also could relate because sacrifice was an essential element of religious practice throughout the Roman Empire.[5] But simply identifying Jesus' execution as an atoning sacrifice would not have made his death seem terribly compelling. It was because Jesus' death was different from, and far superior to, any previous sacrifices that the gospel message took hold of people and turned lives upside down. The language in the New Testament repeatedly points to the earth-shaking uniqueness of Jesus' sacrifice.

Christ's Death: The Incomparable Sacrifice

What made Christ's sacrifice so different from the earlier sacrifices? We must remember that in the animal sacrifices of the Old Testament, several performers played crucial roles in the ritual: *God* instituted the system, accepted the sacrifices, and forgave the sins for which they were offered; a *sinner* provided the victim for the sacrifice and slaughtered it in strict obedience to God's law; the *animal*'s role was simply to die; *priests* were the mediators who presented the blood at the altar.

In Christ's crucifixion it was God, either as Father or as Son, who took every sacrificial role on himself.

It was God, not the sinner, who provided the sacrificial victim, and the offering he brought was far more precious and costly than any offering he had required of his people. "God so loved the world that he gave his one and only Son" (Jn 3:16). He "did not spare his own Son, but gave him up for us all" (Rom 8:32).

In the crucifixion, the Son of God took on the role of victim. Like the sacrificial animals of the Old Testament, he was innocent and without defect. But these earlier victims were, after all, only dumb animals who could not guess what was expected of them as they were led to the altar. Jesus, in contrast, understood completely the terrible agony he would suffer on the cross, as his mental anguish in Gethsemane proved. Yet he gave his life willingly to save sinners: "He humbled himself and became obedient to death—even death on a cross!" (Phil 2:8).

Jesus not only played the role of the victim but the role of priest or mediator as well. And just as he was a victim far superior to those of the old sacrifices, he was a priest far superior to the priests of the old covenant.

Now there have been many of those priests, since death prevented them from continuing in office; but because Jesus lives forever, he has a permanent priesthood. Therefore he is able to save completely those who come to God through him, because he always lives to intercede for them.

Such a high priest meets our need—one who is holy, blameless, pure, set apart from sinners, exalted above the heavens. Unlike the other high priests, he does not need to offer sacrifices day after day, first for his own sins, and then for the sins of the people. He sacrificed for their sins once for all when he offered himself. (Heb 7:23-27)

Can we ever fully grasp the wonder of the cross? Through Christ's sacrifice, God did everything necessary to reconcile sinners to himself. The heavenly Father and the incarnate Son played all the essential roles: provider of the sacrifice, sacrificial victim and priestly mediator. The only part sinful humans played was to slaughter the victim. By killing God's Messiah, they demonstrated that they were proud and unrepentant, helplessly enslaved to sin. Yet Jesus gave his life for sinners before they were ready to acknowledge their need for forgiveness.

Just as the Jews needed to participate in the God-given sacrifice rituals to gain a true sense of their own sinfulness and to experience the goodness of God's mercy, we must become involved imaginatively and emotionally in the New Testament's descriptions of Jesus' crucifixion. As we identify all too easily with the cruelty heaped on Jesus by friend and enemy alike, we become aware of how desperately we ourselves need saving. As we witness the surprising dignity and self-assured purpose—the almost ceremonial quality—of Jesus' dying, we comprehend that he has finished the work that needed to be done to save us.

One climactic detail of the crucifixion drama has particular power to convey the startling new dimensions of God's mercy which Jesus' death has made available. When Christ dies, the curtain in the temple is torn in two (Mt 27:51; Mk 15:38; Lk 23:45). To feel the force of this image, we must be familiar with atoning sacrifice in the Old Testament. That system of sacrifices had kept a "proper" distance between God and his people. God was seen as dwelling in the Holy of Holies, a part of the temple hidden by a heavy curtain, a place so sacred that only the high priest could enter it, and he only once a year on the Day of Atonement. But Christ's death dissolved the distance between God and his sinful creatures.

> *Since we have confidence to enter the Most Holy Place by the blood of Jesus, by a new and living way opened for us through the curtain, that is, his body, and since we have a great priest over the house of God, let us draw near to God with a sincere heart in full assurance of faith. (Heb 10:19-22)*

The Drama of a New Celebration

The graphic language of death, injustice and betrayal mingled with vivid images of ritual sacrifice can draw us into the moving drama of Jesus' sacrificial death. God graciously gave us this powerful language so we could experience his love. But he did not stop there. He knew we would need a concrete way to act out the new relationship with him that Christ's death has made possible, just as the ancient Israelites needed a way to act out God's mercy to them. So Jesus, during the final Passover meal with his disciples, instituted the sacrament of the Lord's Supper. He commanded his followers to repeat this fellowship meal in memory of him.

The ritual meal which Christians have celebrated through

the centuries is similar in some ways to the fellowship meals which often followed Old Testament sacrifices. However, its meaning, suggested in two passages from 1 Corinthians, is far richer than that of the old rituals.

> *Is not the cup of thanksgiving for which we give thanks a participation in the blood of Christ? And is not the bread that we break a participation in the body of Christ? Because there is one loaf, we, who are many, are one body, for we all partake of the one loaf. (1 Cor 10:16-17)*

> *"This is my body, which is for you; do this in remembrance of me. . . . This cup is the new covenant in my blood; do this, whenever you drink it, in remembrance of me." For whenever you eat this bread and drink this cup, you proclaim the Lord's death until he comes. (1 Cor 11:24-26)*

In this sacrament God gives us a way to participate bodily, concretely, in the death of Christ. The Lord's Supper is more than a commemoration and celebration of his sacrifice for us. It is a tangible symbol that Jesus' death in some way nourishes us right now to live in newness of life. The communion meal makes us one with the great fellowship of believers throughout history. And it is a visible anticipation of the even closer fellowship we will enjoy in the kingdom when Christ comes again.

There is no point fooling ourselves that our faith can be more sophisticated, more spiritual than that of the Old Testament believers. Like them we still need to get caught up in the drama of sacrifice. We need to see Jesus as the Lamb whose blood washes away our sins so that we may draw close to God. And we still need tangible rituals to express and embody our faith. That is why God has given us the Lord's Supper, a down-to-earth way to celebrate the amazing closeness to the Almighty which we enjoy because Christ died.

The faith the Bible gives us is always a down-to-earth faith. God did not save us through abstract ideas; he saved us through loving actions played out on the stage of our world. In his Word he tells us the story of his actions in vital literary language. Not just the atonement, but all the great truths of Christianity are encased in powerful imagery and drama. We need to be careful not to drain the Bible of its power by approaching it as a depository of doctrines. Understanding the rational framework of our beliefs is important, but we cannot love a skeleton. In the flesh and blood of the biblical stories and word pictures, we find our living God—Father, Son and Spirit—reaching out to find us and forgive us. Confronted by such tangible mercy, how can we help but respond in love?

Worthy Is the Lamb Who Was Slain:

A Bible Study Focused on a Vision of Heavenly Worship of Our Crucified and Risen Lord

Revelation 5

Please note: Revelation 4:1 begins John's description of a vision in which he is allowed to enter heaven and see the very throne of God. The first few verses of chapter four put Revelation 5 in context.

> *After this I looked, and there before me was a door standing open in heaven. And the voice I had first heard speaking to me like a trumpet said, "Come up here, and I will show you what must take place after this." At once I was in the Spirit, and there before me was a throne in heaven with someone sitting on it. And the one who sat there had the appearance of jasper and carnelian. A rainbow, resembling an emerald, encircled the throne. Surrounding the throne were twenty-four other thrones, and seated on them were twenty-four elders. They were dressed in white and had crowns of gold on their heads. From the throne came flashes of lightning, rumblings and peals of thunder. (Rev 4:1-5)*

1. Read Revelation 5 aloud from three versions of the Bible.

2. Verses 1-4 speak of a scroll which God holds in his hand.

The words of Revelation 4:1 indicate that this scroll will show "what must take place after this." In other words, it will show how God will ultimately work out his purposes of salvation and judgment for the world. Why do you think John weeps when no one can open the scroll and look inside?

3. Verses 5-10 disclose that Jesus Christ is the one who can open the scroll. Jesus is pictured in verse 5 as "the Lion" and in verse 6 as "a Lamb." These pictures are emotionally powerful rather than literally descriptive. What associations and emotions does each image carry for you in relation to Christ? How do they work together to deepen your awareness of who Christ is and what he has done for you?

4. John's vision appeals powerfully to our senses and imaginations as John tries to capture in words the glory and majesty of the divine Father and Son and the perfect worship that is due them. If you were a filmmaker, how would you convey the essence of this scene on the screen? (You may use descriptions from Revelation 4 and 5 that you find moving, but you may also imagine this scene of heavenly worship differently if you think your vision would speak more powerfully to a contemporary audience.)

Consider, for example, how you would visualize the heavenly setting. What lighting effects would you use as the scene develops? How would the participants in the scene (God, Christ and the worshipers) be clothed, and what would their faces look like? What sound effects or background music would you use as the scene unfolds?

5. When the Lamb comes and takes the scroll from God's hand, the response of all present is to worship him (see vv. 8-14). In what different ways do they express their worship? How fully do they participate in the experience?

6. Does this vision of heavenly worship remind you of any worship experiences you yourself have had? Recall what made those experiences moving as the scene in Revelation 5 is moving.

7. Does this passage make you want to worship God and Christ differently than you have been accustomed to worshiping? Explain.

The Mighty One, God, the LORD,
    speaks and summons the earth
    from the rising of the sun to the place where it sets.
From Zion, perfect in beauty,
    God shines forth.
Our God comes and will not be silent;
    a fire devours before him,
    and around him a tempest rages.
He summons the heavens above,
    and the earth, that he may judge his people. (Ps 50:1-4)

7
Powerful Language Puts Us On Trial

G *od judges us, and the whole universe is witness to* his terrible and wonderful judgments. Scenes of courtroom confrontation appear often in the Bible to illustrate God's dealings with humanity. These are dramatic scenes, for the courtroom is an emotionally charged place, a place where issues of right and wrong are decided and people's futures hang in the balance.

We have all seen countless courtroom dramas on TV and in newspapers. Therefore it should not be hard for us to relate to the courtroom scenes in Scripture. Yet at times we may be right in the middle of a trial in the Bible and not realize it, for biblical courtroom drama often provides a backdrop rather than taking center stage. Forensic images or the pattern of legal proceedings may be woven subtly through many paragraphs or chapters to suggest that we are in a courtroom. Unless we read with our minds attuned to imagery, drama and analogy, we may miss the impact of these extended metaphorical trial scenes.

In this chapter we will see that Paul in the first half of Romans, John in his Gospel, and Luke in the book of Acts all make frequent use of courtroom language. As we enter imaginatively into this language, we become aware that no matter what else is happening in the foreground of these books, in the background a court case of cosmic significance is being tried and issues of eternal consequence are being decided.

We will probably be surprised at the difference a sensitivity to courtroom drama makes in our reading of these familiar New Testament books. It may seem as if we have put on special glasses to view a 3-D movie. As the trial images jump out at us, we find ourselves drawn into the action. Suddenly we are on trial. The metaphoric language of the courtroom grips not only our emotions, but our intellects and wills as well. We are compelled to decide what we believe, who we will follow, how we will respond.

Before we can plunge fully into the courtroom atmosphere of Romans, John and Acts, it will be helpful to review a few features of the Old Testament understanding of divine and human justice.

God As Judge, People As Witnesses

The Old Testament portrays God as judge over the whole earth, but he never appears as an aloof, impassive magistrate. God is always personally and passionately involved with issues of right and wrong in his world.

The justice of God in the Old Testament has two faces. One aspect of God's justice is stern and perfectly fair, demanding that people be rewarded if they are good and punished if they are wicked. The other side of God's justice is compassionate, desiring that the poor be provided for, the powerless be protected and the sinful be granted mercy. These two expressions of justice—giving people what they deserve and giving people what they need—always coexist in God's nature and define what it means for him to be a just judge. The wrath of God must fall on people because they are sinners; the love of God must reach out to people because they are needy.

God's passionate concern for justice, and the condemning and compassionate aspects of his justice, are captured in the legal codes of the Old Testament. We can see them clearly in the following passage, where God says to his people:

Do not take advantage of a widow or an orphan. If you do and they cry out to me, I will certainly hear their cry. My anger will be aroused, and I will kill you with the sword; your wives will become widows and your children fatherless. (Ex 22:22-24)

Naturally God demands that the legal proceedings of his people reflect his own justice. In his law he emphasizes the importance of honest testimony in court.

Do not spread false reports. Do not help a wicked man by being a malicious witness.

Do not follow the crowd in doing wrong. When you give testimony in a lawsuit, do not pervert justice by siding with the crowd, and do not show favoritism. . . .

Have nothing to do with a false charge and do not put an innocent or honest person to death, for I will not acquit the guilty.

Do not accept a bribe, for a bribe blinds those who see and twists the words of the righteous. (Ex 23:1-3, 7-8)

Witnesses played a more decisive role in the legal system of ancient Israel than they play in trials today. The courts we read about in the Old Testament did not employ professional prosecutors or defense lawyers. Witnesses not only gave objective information, they also acted as advocates who interpreted the facts and argued for their cause. Often cases were won, not when a panel of judges handed down a ruling, but when the witnesses on one side presented such persuasive arguments that their opponents were silenced.[1]

God recognized the danger that false witnesses could pervert justice, so he built safeguards into his law to help see that justice was done. The most important of these was the requirement of multiple witnesses to establish any cause.

> *One witness is not enough to convict a man accused of any crime or offense he may have committed. A matter must be established by the testimony of two or three witnesses. (Deut 19:15)*

The New Testament writers followed the Old Testament in insisting that God's wrath against the wicked and his compassion for the needy were essential to his just nature. They also stressed the importance of human witnesses and reaffirmed the principle that there must be at least two witnesses to establish any cause. With an awareness of these important concepts from the Old Testament that flow into the New, we are ready to respond to the courtroom drama in Romans, John and Acts.

A Just God Deals with Sinners

Paul's concept of justification is at heart a forensic metaphor. Paul pictures all people standing before God the judge, sentenced to death because of their sin. However, because Christ takes the punishment they deserve, they can stand before God justified (acquitted) and enjoy eternal life.

This concept is presented most fully in the first eight chapters of Romans. We have probably been taught to view these chapters as a tightly reasoned treatise on our need for salvation and God's strategy to save us. However, they will involve us more effectively if we realize that Paul's language and the progression of his thought actually summon us into the dramatic world of the courtroom, where we find ourselves standing before God, the righteous judge of the universe.

In Romans 1—3 Paul acts as a prosecuting attorney speaking on behalf of God. Romans 1:18-32 is his thundering opening statement in which he delineates both the charges God brings against sinful people and the punishment that is due them. Because their idolatry and immorality constitute convincing proof that they have turned against God, "the wrath of God" falls upon them as he "gives them over" to be imprisoned in their own depravity and deluded thinking.[2]

During this opening statement, Paul allows his readers to remain complacent spectators at the trial. He directs his accusations at "them," all those "other" people who are guilty of sexual perversion and idolatry and all manner of other sins. Even if some of the crimes Paul mentions sound uncomfortably familiar (envy, for instance, and gossip and boasting), the charges are not leveled at us. But in chapter 2 Paul turns to every spectator, every reader, and says:

You, therefore, have no excuse, you who pass judgment on someone else, for at whatever point you judge the other, you are condemning yourself, because you who pass judgment do the same things.

But because of your stubbornness and your unrepentant heart, you are storing up wrath against yourself for the day of God's wrath, when his righteous judgment will be revealed. (Rom 2:1, 5)

The effect is the same as if we were simply sitting in on a trial and the prosecutor suddenly unleashed on us all the accusations and denunciations he had been directing at the defendant.

By chapter 3, Paul has included everyone in his charges, including himself.

What shall we conclude then? Are we any better? Not at all! We have already made the charge that Jews and Gentiles alike are all under sin. As it is written:

"There is no one righteous, not even one." (Rom 3:9-10)

Paul's devastating conclusion as prosecuting attorney: Everyone has broken God's law, and "no one will be declared righteous in his sight by observing the law" (Rom 3:20).

At this point in Romans, we can feel a deadly hush fall over the courtroom. The judge of the universe has focused his terrible gaze on every spectator, every witness, every lawyer, and "every mouth [is] silenced" (Rom 3:19) as they realize there is nothing they can say in their defense.

Then the great reversal in the book of Romans occurs. While the guilty await their just punishment, new, surprising evidence is introduced. Paul testifies to this evidence:

But now a righteousness from God, apart from law, has been made known, to which the Law and the Prophets testify. This righteousness from God comes through faith in Jesus Christ to all who believe. . . . God presented him as a sacrifice of atonement. . . . He did this . . . to demonstrate his justice at the present time, so as to be just and the one who justifies those who have faith in Jesus. (Rom 3:21-26)

The first three chapters of Romans force us to look at the hard face of God's justice. All people have chosen to reject God's rule, and his stern righteousness demands that they pay the penalty for their sin. But in chapters 4—7 of Romans, Paul conveys the sense that God is now turning his loving face to us. God becomes the merciful judge who sees people as help-less victims of sin and reaches out to rescue them. Paul explains:

> *You see, at just the right time, when we were still powerless, Christ died for the ungodly. God demonstrates his own love for us in this: While we were still sinners, Christ died for us. (Rom 5:6, 8)*

In Christ's death God's need to punish sin has been satisfied, and his compassionate determination to rescue the oppressed is fulfilled as well.

In Romans 5—7 Paul repeatedly pictures God, through his Son, being the deliverer of those who are victimized by sin. Jesus' dying has overthrown the tyrant, death, which has reigned over people since Adam's fall (see Rom 5:12-21). Though all people have been cruelly enslaved by sin, Christ's crucifixion has freed them from their bondage (see Rom 6—7). Romans 8 is Paul's summation, his resounding testimony to the rescuing, merciful side of God's justice. In this chapter Paul's repeated use of forensic language draws us again into a court-room scene, as it did in chapters 1—3, but a change has occurred in the courtroom atmosphere! Now God the judge stands with us in our weakness and passes judgment on sin and death which have been oppressing us. Jesus Christ and the Holy Spirit act as witnesses in our defense.

> *Therefore, there is now no condemnation for those who are in Christ Jesus, because through Christ Jesus the law of the Spirit of life set me free from the law of sin and death. For what the law was powerless to do, . . . God did by sending his own Son in the likeness of sinful man to be a sin offering. And so he condemned sin in sinful man, in order that the righteous requirements of the law might be fully met in us. (Rom 8:1-4)*

The Spirit himself testifies with our spirit that we are God's children. (Rom 8:16)

The Spirit helps us in our weakness. We do not know what we ought to pray for, but the Spirit himself intercedes for us. . . . (Rom 8:26)

If God is for us, who can be against us? He who did not spare his own Son, but gave him up for us all—how will he not also, along with him, graciously give us all things? Who will bring any charge against those whom God has chosen? It is God who justifies. Who is he that condemns? Christ Jesus, who died—more than that, who was raised to life—is at the right hand of God and is also interceding for us. (Rom 8:31-34)

As we read the first eight chapters of Paul's epistle to the Romans, we are caught off guard by the surprising turns this metaphorical trial takes. Starting as spectators, we quickly find ourselves on trial, accused and condemned. But Christ's unexpected sacrifice wins our pardon, and at the same time shatters the sin and death which have held us captive. In Christ we find we are God's cherished children who stand under the judge's special protection while he condemns our oppressors.

The courtroom drama in Romans should terrify us, then delight us. But its impact on us will depend on whether or not we allow the powerful language to draw us in. Will we acknowledge that we are among the guilty who deserve punishment by a just God? Will we confess that we are among the helpless who must depend on God's grace for salvation? It is possible to read Romans as bystanders, students, analysts, and hold Paul's persuasive testimony at a distance. But if we remain spectators, we will not find the life and joy that are described so movingly in Romans 8.

Christ and the World Are on Trial

If Paul lets us view theology through the lens of courtroom metaphor, John encourages us to view historical events through that same lens. The prologue of John's Gospel immediately establishes the adversarial tone of the book. John sets forth light opposed by darkness, the Word (Jesus Christ) opposed by the world, belief opposed by unbelief.

In the Gospel of John, almost all of Jesus' confrontations with people are presented in a trial atmosphere with Jesus as the focal point of judgment: people judge Jesus, even as they also are judged. John uses forensic language to stress his theme that each person's eternal destiny will depend on a response to Jesus.

God did not send his Son into the world to condemn *the world, but to save the world through him. Whoever believes in him is not* con-demned, *but whoever does not believe* stands condemned *already because he has not believed in the name of God's one and only Son. This is the* verdict: *Light has come into the world, but men loved darkness instead of light because their deeds were evil. (Jn 3:17-19)*

As we read through John's Gospel keeping our eyes peeled for courtroom patterns and our ears tuned to forensic speech, we see a trial atmosphere being created in three ways. First, John uses forensic terminology as he demonstrates that various witnesses testify that Jesus is the Savior. Second, a contentious tone pervades the book as Jesus' opponents accuse and question him and he accuses and questions them in turn. Third, "physical evidence" in the form of Jesus' miracles or signs is introduced at intervals to prove that he is who he says he is. In the first twelve chapters of John, these three components of a court case appear so often that we can hardly forget we are sitting in on a trial.

A crucial question occurs to us: "Who, exactly, is on trial in

John's Gospel?" In one sense Jesus is clearly on trial. He is the accused. Those who wield religious power in Israel—the Pharisees, priests and scribes whom John often refers to simply as "the Jews"—are continually trying to prove that Jesus is flouting God's laws and deserves to die. Jesus must defend himself against their charges.

In another sense, the Jews themselves are really the ones on trial. God has sent his Son to bring light to the world, and as Jesus shines the light of God's truth on the Jewish leaders, their foolishness, duplicity, ambition and fear are exposed. Jesus warns them that if they reject him, they will be condemned and will die in their sins.

The prologue of John's Gospel immediately suggests a courtroom atmosphere by calling John the Baptist a witness rather than a prophet. The narrative itself begins with John being questioned and giving testimony, thus plunging us right into a trial scenario.

> *Now this was John's testimony when the Jews of Jerusalem sent priests and Levites to ask him who he was. He did not fail to confess, but confessed freely, "I am not the Christ."*
>
> *They asked him, "Then who are you? Are you Elijah?"*
>
> *He said, "I am not."*
>
> *"Are you the Prophet?"*
>
> *He answered, "No."*
>
> *Finally they said, "Who are you? Give us an answer to take back to those who sent us. What do you say about yourself?"*
>
> *John replied in the words of Isaiah the prophet, "I am the voice of one calling in the desert, 'Make straight the way for the Lord.' "*
>
> *Now some Pharisees who had been sent questioned him, "Why then do you baptize if you are not the Christ, nor Elijah, nor the Prophet?"* (Jn 1:19-24)

Already in this first exchange we see the lines drawn between the opposing sides in the courtroom battle, with the Jewish establishment confronting John, Christ's representative. The forensic vocabulary is here—"testimony," "confessed," "questioned"—as well as the question-and-answer format that is typical of a trial.

When Jesus appears the next day at the Jordan, John the Baptist points him out—"Look, the Lamb of God, who takes away the sin of the world! This is the one I meant" (Jn 1:29-30). Doesn't this sound exactly like a witness pointing out in court the person he has been testifying about? John goes on to say, "I saw the Spirit come down from heaven as a dove and remain on him. I have seen and I testify that this is the Son of God" (Jn 1:32, 34). He is emphasizing that he is an eyewitness who has seen evidence that proves what he says is true.

The following sentences tell how John's testimony results in some of his disciples deciding to follow Jesus. Soon after, Jesus performs a miracle, changing water to wine at a wedding. The author of the book comments, "This, the first of his miraculous signs, Jesus performed in Cana of Galilee. He thus revealed his glory, and his disciples put their faith in him" (Jn 2:11). Note how John carefully labels this miracle as to when and where it was performed. He sounds very much like an attorney saying, "Your honor, I now enter in evidence Exhibit One." This pattern continues in John's Gospel. Interspersed with reports of the testimony given by Jesus and others, John inserts accounts of Jesus' miracles which serve as visible corroboration that he is the Messiah. This "physical evidence" is introduced to call forth faith in those who see, just as the words of all who testify to Christ are designed to call forth faith in those who hear.

As John's Gospel unfolds, Jesus' opponents regularly question him, thus giving him the opportunity to testify about himself. Jesus makes a special point of stressing that his testimony can be believed because he himself is an eyewitness to the spiritual realities he teaches. He comes from heaven and has seen God (see Jn 3:11-13; 6:46-50). Jesus also stresses that his testimony is credible because it conforms to the Old Testament requirement for multiple witnesses. John the Baptist has testified to who he is, and so have the Scriptures and the miracles he has performed. Jesus' care to defend his credibility as a witness is demonstrated in this exchange with his accusers.

The Pharisees challenged him, "Here you are, appearing as your own witness; your testimony is not valid."

Jesus answered, "Even if I testify on my own behalf, my testimony is valid, for I know where I came from and where I am going. . . . I am not alone. I stand with the Father who sent me. In your own Law it is written that the testimony of two men is valid. I am one who testifies for myself; my other witness is the Father who sent me." (Jn 8:13-18)

As John's account proceeds, more and more people are swayed by Jesus' forceful words. In the face of his powerful testimony the questioning of his opponents appears inept. Unable to make any charge stick, they try violent means to silence Jesus, but even these attempts fail miserably.

Again the Jews picked up stones to stone him, but Jesus said to them, "I have shown you many great miracles from the Father. For which of these do you stone me?"

"We are not stoning you for any of these," replied the Jews, "but for blasphemy, because you, a mere man, claim to be God."

Jesus answered them, . . ."Why then do you accuse me of blasphemy because I said, 'I am God's Son'? Do not believe me unless I do what my Father does. But if I do it, even though you do not believe me, believe the miracles, that you may know and understand that the Father is in me, and I in the Father." Again they tried to seize him, but he escaped their grasp. (Jn 10:31-39)

An exchange like the one above shows that Jesus clearly has the upper hand in this metaphorical trial. He does not just defend himself; he accuses his accusers, exposing their guilt and passing sentence on them. One time when the Pharisees challenge him, he tells them:

"You are from below; I am from above. You are of this world; I am not of this world. I told you that you would die in your sins; if you do not believe that I am the one I claim to be, you will indeed die in your sins." *(Jn 8:23-24)*

In the heated courtroom atmosphere of John 1—12, it is not only Jesus' words that put his opponents to shame. The "physical evidence" he presents in the form of compassionate actions toward others makes his adversaries' self-serving behavior appear especially despicable. For example, when the teachers of the law and Pharisees publicly accuse the woman taken in adultery in order to trap Jesus, his staunch defense and gentle forgiveness of the woman stand in glaring contrast to the cruel way they have exploited her for their own ends.

By chapter 12, the metaphorical trial between Jesus and his enemies has built to a climax. After his triumphal entry into Jerusalem, they have to admit, "See, this is getting us nowhere. Look how the whole world has gone after him!" (Jn 12:19). Most of the Jewish establishment still refuse to believe in him, "yet at the same time many even among the leaders believed in him" (Jn 12:42). It would seem Jesus has won his case. Yet he speaks as if he is going to withdraw from the world rather than enjoy his victory. "You are going to have the light just a little while longer," he tells his listeners (Jn 12:35).

After chapter 12 there is an interlude in the courtroom atmosphere of the book as Jesus gathers with his disciples to prepare them for his death. In a sense this too heightens the drama, almost as if the jury is out and we are waiting for their verdict. Then in John 18 Jesus is arrested and we are plunged back into a courtroom atmosphere in the actual trials of Jesus, first before Annas and Caiaphas, then before the Roman governor.

Even in these trials, though they lead to execution, Jesus clearly triumphs. The Jewish leaders cannot make a single charge stick. No witnesses are called against him. In effect Jesus has silenced his opponents, proof that he has won his case.[3] Later Pilate actually testifies for him, saying three times, "I find no basis for a charge against him" (Jn 18:38; 19:4, 6). Only by blatantly perverting justice, by breaking all their own rules, can the Jews and the Romans put Jesus to death.

In killing Jesus the Jews think they have won. But of course there is a wonderful irony here. Even as Jesus dies, he accomplishes the very purpose for which he came to earth, winning life for all who believe in him. His resurrection is the last act in the courtroom drama between Jesus and the worldly Jews. It is the final overwhelming piece of physical evidence presented in John. Jesus had said that he would rise from the grave (Jn 2:18-22), and his rising is the incontrovertible proof that he is indeed the Son of God, the light of men who has the power to bring life to all who believe.

As we become attuned to the courtroom atmosphere of John, hearing Jesus' opponents accuse and question him, listening to the testimony on Jesus' behalf and seeing the evidence of his miracles, it is difficult to remain impartial observers. The fact that John stages Jesus' ministry as a trial catches us up in the necessity to take sides. We are called on to judge, required to reach a verdict about Jesus.

Every element in John's Gospel propels us toward the right verdict. John structures his drama around the kind of persuasive arguments we would expect to hear in court. We are invited to weigh the testimony and the evidence rationally and reach a decision about Jesus. But John's courtroom drama also works on our feelings. Jesus' opponents are shown to be such inept bunglers, so blind and self-serving, that we despise them. In contrast, Jesus comes across as so gracious and vulnerable that we long to take his side. God in Jesus has surrendered himself to the world, allowed the world to bring him to trial. His love for all people shines brightly in John's Gospel as he pleads, argues, advances proofs to win over his opponents. Jesus says repeatedly that he does not want to judge them, but wants them to gain eternal life. Finally he proves his great love by dying for them.

Nevertheless, judgment will come for those who do not judge Jesus rightly. Jesus warns, "There is a judge for the one who rejects me and does not accept my words; that very word which I spoke will condemn him at the last day" (Jn 12:48). Any unbeliever who reads John's Gospel is faced squarely with the choice: Will I put my faith in Jesus Christ, or not?

The Trial Continues in Acts

If John's Gospel presents a powerful case for faith in Christ, Luke's challenge in Acts is directed more at the person who already believes. The book opens with Jesus' charge to the disciples before he ascends to heaven: "You will receive power when the Holy Spirit comes on you; and you will be my witnesses in Jerusalem, and in all Judea and Samaria, and to the ends of the earth" (Acts 1:8).

Jesus' words indicate that the trial is not over. The same

confrontation that he carried on with the world in John's Gospel must now be carried on by his followers. For although Jesus won the victory over sin and death in his crucifixion and resurrection, God is withholding the final judgment until as many as possible can be saved. Jesus counts on his followers to testify to the world, just as he did, to try to win them to salvation.

If we go back to the book of John, we see how even before his death Jesus began to prepare his disciples for their ongoing role as witnesses. "You also must testify," he told them, "for you have been with me from the beginning" (Jn 15:27). Jesus assured his disciples that the world's response to their witnessing would be the same as the response Jesus had already received. People would be divided. Some would be convinced and believe, but many would hate and reject them, just as they had hated and rejected him (see Jn 15:20). Yet Jesus promised them wonderful help in the trials they would face. They would not stand alone, for he would send them the Counselor, the Holy Spirit.

The Greek word translated "Counselor" in the New International Version actually means an advocate, one who defends someone else in a courtroom. This choice of words highlights the function of the Holy Spirit as one who helps believers in their role as witnesses for Jesus Christ in the world. Jesus told his disciples:

"All this I have spoken while still with you. But the Counselor, the Holy Spirit, whom the Father will send in my name, will teach you all things and will remind you of everything I have said to you. (Jn 14:25-26)

"When the Counselor comes, whom I will send to you from the Father, the Spirit of truth who goes out from the Father, he will testify about me.

And you also must testify." (Jn 15:26-27)

When [the Counselor] comes, he will convict the world of guilt in regard to sin and righteousness and judgment: in regard to sin, because men do not believe in me; in regard to righteousness, because I am going to the Father, where you can see me no longer; and in regard to judgment, because the prince of this world now stands condemned. (Jn 16:8-11)

Note that in these verses both the disciples and the world are pictured as being on trial. Jesus assured his disciples that when the world called them to account, the Holy Spirit would be standing with them to help them testify effectively and to convict those listening of their own guilt and of the truth of the gospel message.

When we read the book of Acts, we can see quite clearly that Jesus' followers are continuing the court battle that occupied Jesus in the book of John. The trial is in a new stage, however. During Christ's ministry on earth he foretold how his death, resurrection and glorification would win salvation for sinners. In Acts his followers testify that they have witnessed Jesus' death, resurrection and ascension—which proves that he has already won eternal life for sinners. Furthermore, whereas Jesus stressed that the Father stood with him, in Acts his disciples emphasize their reliance on the Holy Spirit within them to back up their witness. As Peter and the other apostles testify:

The God of our fathers raised Jesus from the dead—whom you had killed by hanging him on a tree. God exalted him to his own right hand as Prince and Savior that he might give repentance and forgiveness of sins to Israel. We are witnesses of these things, and so is the Holy Spirit, whom God has given to those who obey him." (Acts 5:30-32)

If anything, the courtroom atmosphere in Acts confronts us

more directly than the similar atmosphere in John. This is partly because Luke's account includes over a dozen instances in which one or more of the early Christians were actually arrested and brought to trial because of their faith. Some of the most effective preaching of the good news in Acts occurs in actual courtrooms or similar forums.[4]

Luke clearly demonstrates that when Christians are brought to trial it is part of God's plan, a great opportunity for them to testify to Christ. When Paul defends himself before King Agrippa, the ruler recognizes that Paul has been using the hearing as an opportunity to try to win him to faith, and Paul readily acknowledges this.

> *Then Agrippa said to Paul, "Do you think that in such a short time you can persuade me to be a Christian?"*
>
> *Paul replied, "Short time or long—I pray God that not only you but all who are listening to me today may become what I am, except for these chains." (Acts 26:28-29)*

The outcome of the courtroom proceedings pictured in Acts serves as proof that God is the ultimate judge in control of the world. When Christians speak boldly before human courts, God always sees that his cause will be advanced, no matter how antagonistic the human accusers or magistrates are. For example, when Stephen is arrested, tried and stoned for his faith, the ensuing persecution scatters the Jerusalem Christians who then preach the gospel in new places (see Acts 7:59—8:4). When the Jews in Jerusalem bring Paul to trial, he ends up in Rome, just where God wanted him, preaching "boldly and without hindrance" (see Acts 28:31).[5]

Even when the Christians in Acts are not formally on trial, we can see that a courtroom atmosphere surrounds their witness as it surrounded Jesus' ministry. The similarities between the dramas in Acts and John are startling.

At Iconium Paul and Barnabas went as usual into the Jewish synagogue. There they spoke so effectively that a great number of Jews and Gentiles believed. But the Jews who refused to believe stirred up the Gentiles and poisoned their minds against the brothers. So Paul and Barnabas spent considerable time there, speaking boldly for the Lord, who confirmed the message of his grace by enabling them to do miraculous signs and wonders. The people of the city were divided; some sided with the Jews, others with the apostles. There was a plot afoot among the Gentiles and Jews, together with their leaders, to mistreat them and stone them. But they found out about it and fled to the Lycaonian cities of Lystra and Derbe and to the surrounding country, where they continued to preach the good news (Acts 14:1-7).

Here, as in John's Gospel, is the contentious atmosphere of a trial, but now the disciples are playing the role Jesus played. They boldly testify in the face of opposition from the leaders of the society. There are multiple witnesses to the truth, Paul and Barnabas testifying together, and the miracles they perform serve as physical evidence to corroborate what they say. Their testimony brings belief, but also division. Their opponents cannot effectively counter their arguments verbally, so must resort to violence. Yet their adversaries' plots cannot stop the spread of the truth which God and his Holy Spirit empower. In fact persecution simply magnifies their effectiveness, just as Jesus' death allowed him to achieve the purpose for which God sent him.

The narrative of Acts provides convincing evidence that Christ's followers cannot lose their case. In the Holy Spirit's power, Christian witness will go forward. What Jesus prophesied for his disciples in the first chapter of Acts actually happens, as the good news spreads inexorably outward from

Jerusalem. Clearly Christians have the upper hand in their confrontation with the world. They are already sure of their own verdict of acquittal before God through the death and resurrection of Jesus Christ. It is the fate of their accusers that hangs in the balance. In fact, their worldly accusers are actually the ones on trial. But the Christians who witness to them are not any more anxious to judge them than their Master was. Instead they hope to win these opponents to Christ and the life he offers.

When we as Christians enter imaginatively into the courtroom drama that pervades the book of Acts, we recognize that our lives are a continuation of the trial portrayed there. God is still withholding his final judgment so that more people can be saved. Christ has given us the great privilege and responsibility of testifying on his behalf to those who do not know him or accept him.

Listening to the courageous testimony of the first Christians calls us to account. Are we as excited about what Jesus has done for us as Peter and Paul were? Do we love the unsaved world enough to share our faith with them? Knowing that God is in charge when we face the world and that his Spirit is standing with us, do we speak out boldly? Or do we retreat into safe silence, even when the world does not openly accuse us or mock us or persecute us? These are the questions the book of Acts asks us.

Breadth and Depth of Vision

Tuning in to the metaphorical trials woven through Romans, John and Acts, we realize that the excitement of these dramas, like that of real-life courtroom confrontations, builds slowly. We cannot feel their full impact unless we are willing to sit patiently and attend carefully while events unfold. Focusing on a few verses or a single chapter will not give us the perspective we need. But when we broaden our vision by reading several chapters at once, we can begin to grasp the terrible and wonderful truth that our God is judging the world, even as he solicits its judgment.

The extended trial scenes in these three books also demonstrate the need for us to look deep into ourselves when we read the Bible. In Romans, John and Acts, we are on trial before God and before the world. The truth of who we are is being exposed. What do we really believe? Who have we chosen to follow? How well do our speech and actions testify to our faith?

Exploring the courtroom dramas in the New Testament reminds us that the powerful literary language in the Bible is not only God's gift to us, but also his summons, his command. "Surrender," it says to us. "God is the mighty Judge and Savior. Put your lives in his hands."

Christians Called to Account:

A Bible Study Focused on Courtroom Drama

Acts 4:1-31

Please note: As the fourth chapter of Acts opens, Peter and John have just healed a crippled beggar at the gate of the temple, and many Jews are now listening to their preaching with great interest. You may want to read Acts 3 before reading the assigned passage for this week.

1. Read Acts 4:1-31 aloud from two different versions of the Bible. Does the story capture your attention and get you involved? If so, can you explain why?

2. Among the men trying Peter and John were Annas, Caiaphas and certainly several of the others who had tried Jesus only months before. How do you think the two disciples felt when they were brought before these men for questioning?

3. Drama appeals principally to our emotions. Few emotions are actually named in this passage, but many emotions are implied in the words or indicated by the actions of the various players in the drama. As you read through the passage, guess what emotions probably accompanied each speech or action. You may want to note your guesses.

4. What is your emotional response to each of the players in the drama—the Jewish leaders, Peter and John, and the other believers who appear in verses 23-31? Can you think of actors or other public personalities whom you would cast in these various roles if you were going to produce this story on stage?

5. What kinds of conflict do you see operating in this account? Internal conflict? Conflict between people? Conflict between ideas or principles? Define what the specific conflicts are.

6. Does the way the Jewish leaders reacted to Peter and John's preaching remind you of the way our society reacts to Christian witness today? Why or why not? Do you yourself ever react similarly to Christians who witness boldly? Explain.

7. Have you recently found yourself in a situation where you felt you were on trial because you were a Christian? Were you questioned or called to account for your actions or threatened in some way? What specifically was the situation? How did you respond to the confrontation?

8. When you read this account, do you feel that it puts you on trial? What questions does it lead you to ask yourself? Does it convict you and challenge you to change in any way? Explain.

"Can a mother forget the baby at her breast
    and have no compassion on the child she has borne?
Though she may forget,
    I will not forget you!" (Is 49:15)

"For I am the LORD, your God,
    who takes hold of your right hand
and says to you, Do not fear;
    I will help you.
Do not be afraid, O worm Jacob,
    O little Israel,
for I myself will help you," declares the LORD. (Is 41:13-14)

8
Reading God's Word in God's Family

*O*ur God is never distant or detached from his human creatures. Continually he reaches out to take hold of us. His desire to draw close to us and love us was perfectly embodied in Christ the living Word, but it is also expressed in the literary power of his written Word. Throughout this book, we have explored the gracious way God "speaks our language" in the Bible, employing stories and word pictures from our earthly experience in order to touch us at every level of our beings.

The preceding chapters have highlighted several categories of imagery and drama—images of animals, water and the human body; dramas of birth, death, temple sacrifice and courtroom confrontation. Along the way we have met language that pointed us to other metaphorical worlds we haven't had time to explore—among them the worlds of agriculture, military strategy and music. It has become abundantly clear how crucial it is for us to tune in to literary language if we really want to hear God speaking to us in the Bible. In this final chapter we will review various ways to enter imaginatively and emotionally into the biblical text.

This chapter revolves around imagery of family relationships. In the opening quotations from Isaiah, God compares himself to a mother gazing tenderly at her nursing infant and to a father reaching down his big hand to reassure a frightened toddler. Many of the passages we will explore in the following pages portray God as parent and people as his children. Highlighting these parent-child pictures will reinforce the central theme of this book: God wants to touch us personally through his Word, wrapping his accepting arms around us while prodding us to grow up.

After we have focused on several parent-child images in the Bible, we will turn to family imagery with a somewhat different slant. Much New Testament language reminds us that as Christians we are not just God's children; we are also brothers and sisters to one another. Such imagery suggests one final, crucial guideline for reading the Bible. Important as it is to learn how to read Scripture individually and hear God's personal message to us, we must always remember the benefits of reading God's Word in the context of Christian community.

Old Testament Pictures of God the Father

Moses told the Israelites, "You are the children of the LORD your God. . . . Out of all the peoples on the face of the earth, the LORD has chosen you to be his treasured possession" (Deut 14:1-2). The New Testament teaches that Christians are "Abraham's seed" and the church is the new Israel, so we know that Moses' words apply to us too.[1] Therefore, we will want to *listen carefully to the rich nuances of the words,* being sensitive to the associations they carry. The impact of words like *children, chosen* and *treasured* expands far beyond their dictionary definitions. They can fill in empty places in our hearts, speaking to our deep desires to belong, to be special to someone, to be part of a family.

Repeatedly in the Old Testament, family metaphors are used to describe the ongoing relationship between God and his chosen people. Through his prophet Hosea, God recalls how he rescued Israel and led the toddler nation into the Promised Land, and how they repaid him for his tender care.

"When Israel was a child, I loved him,
   and out of Egypt I called my son.
But the more I called Israel,
   the further they went from me.
They sacrificed to the Baals
   and they burned incense to images.
It was I who taught Ephraim to walk,
   taking them by the arms;
but they did not realize
   it was I who healed them.
I led them with cords of human kindness,
   with ties of love;
I lifted the yoke from their neck
   and bent down to feed them. (Hos 11:1-4)

One way to hear this kind of emotion-packed language better is to *imagine the tones of voice behind the words.* In this passage God reminisces over his child Israel, remembering when the nation was newly freed from Egypt. We can almost hear his voice tremble with unshed tears as he recalls how Israel, weak and wobbly, turned to him for help. But we can hear an angry edge in God's words too. His child has been ungrateful, heartless and downright stupid to reject his love and go after false gods.

In Deuteronomy the wayward Israel (Jeshurun) is pictured as a child who has "grown too big for his britches."

Jeshurun grew fat and kicked;
   filled with food, he became heavy and sleek.
He abandoned the God who made him
   and rejected the Rock his Savior.
You deserted the Rock, who fathered you;
   you forgot the God who gave you birth. (Deut 32:15, 18)

Metaphoric language can often speak more forcefully to us if we *explore how the images may apply to our current culture or circumstances.* When I read of a nation grown fat and full, I think of our society, which spends millions on convenience foods and more millions on weight-loss programs. Is it because we are preoccupied with consuming countless goods and services, I wonder, that we so easily forget the God who has blessed us with such abundance?

In Hosea God reveals that in spite of Israel's rejection of him, he will not abandon his people. His love for them is too strong.

"How can I give you up, Ephraim?
   How can I hand you over, Israel? . . .
My heart is changed within me;
   all my compassion is aroused.
I will not carry out my fierce anger,
   nor will I turn and devastate Ephraim.
For I am God, and not man—
   the Holy One among you.
I will not come in wrath.
They will follow the LORD;
   he will roar like a lion.

When he roars,
  his children will come trembling from the west.
They will come trembling
  like birds from Egypt,
  like doves from Assyria.
I will settle them in their homes,"
  declares the LORD. *(Hos 11:8-11)*

This passage provides a wonderful window into the heart of God. Its words can find a home in our hearts if we *let the language evoke personal memories and longings* in us.

One evening in a small group, a couple gave me new insights into the depths of love expressed in this passage when they shared a story about their only daughter. She had run away at the age of fourteen. Though they discovered where she was, she refused to come home for months. Emotionally, she shut them out for years. Yet her cruel treatment of them could not extinguish their love for her. Their painful memories allowed them to enter into God's hurt far more fully than I could. Reading the same passage, I found I could identify more with God's hope than with his hurt. As he took pleasure in picturing the time when his people would return to him, I often find joy in visualizing how people I pray for will one day find their way back to the God they have rejected.

When we open ourselves to the language of these Old Testament passages, the ancient words can give us fresh perspective on our present world and help us to know better our own heart's longings, fears and rebelliousness. Furthermore, they show us the heart of our divine Father, who binds himself to his creatures with "cords of love," who delights in their growth and who is wounded by their defiance.

In spite of the way these parent-child images touch us, however, we sense a certain distance in the relationship they portray. God in the Old Testament revealed himself as Father of the *nation* Israel (also called Ephraim, Zion and Jeshurun). Nowhere in the verses above are *individuals* encouraged to address God as Father. His titles remain awesome: "the Lord your God," "the God who gave you birth," "the Holy One among you." The Old Testament Father-God, while passionate in his love for his people, remained in many ways a stern, intimidating parent. In the New Testament we see how Jesus opened up the possibility of a closer relationship between people and their heavenly Father.

A New Intimacy with the Father

No single word in the New Testament captures so clearly the way Jesus altered our relationship with God as the word *Father*. Jesus' life and death taught us we can call God "our Father." We have grown so accustomed to thinking and speaking of God this way that we easily forget the magnitude of what we are saying. Through Christ we really do have a new, never-before-possible intimacy with the Lord of the universe.

While Jesus lived on this earth, he modeled this intimacy for us. At his baptism he heard God assuring him, "You are my Son, whom I love; with you I am well pleased" (Mk 1:11); throughout his ministry there was never a break in the communion between him and his Father. Jesus addressed God in prayer as "Father" and was confident that his Father heard him.[2]

Probably Jesus always used the Aramaic word *abba* when he spoke to God, and also used this term in public when speaking of his Father.[3] *Abba* was a completely unceremonious word that had the ring of close family warmth and affection, a word like *daddy* in our culture. Since Christians take intimacy with God for granted, it's hard for us to imagine how Jesus' use of this word must have affected his countrymen.

In the Gospel of John we read of the Jews' violent reaction to Jesus calling God "abba."

> *Jesus said to them, "My Father is always at his work to this very day, and I, too, am working." For this reason the Jews tried all the harder to kill him; not only was he breaking the Sabbath, but he was even calling God his own Father, making himself equal with God. (Jn 5:17-18)*

When we meet Jesus' opponents in the gospel accounts, we tend to dismiss them as narrow-minded, evil-hearted men. But in fact they saw themselves as defending the honor and holiness of God. Perhaps, hearing Jesus call God "daddy," they felt outraged as many Christians now feel when a book or movie popularizes the person of Christ. If we take the time to *put ourselves in the heads and hearts of the people we read about in Scripture,* trying to understand their feelings and motives, we will experience God's Word speaking more dynamically to us. In the case of the verses above, we may comprehend as never before how truly shocking is the grace God extends to us: imagine the ruler of the universe inviting us to call him "Daddy"!

The John 5 passage continues by telling us Jesus' response to the Jews' outrage.

> *Jesus gave them this answer: "I tell you the truth, the Son can do nothing by himself; he can do only what he sees his Father doing, because whatever the Father does the Son also does. For the Father loves the Son and shows him all he does. Yes, to your amazement he will show him even greater things than these. For just as the Father raises the dead and gives them life, even so the Son gives life to whom he is pleased to give it. Moreover, the Father judges no one, but has entrusted all judgment to the Son, that*

all may honor the Son just as they honor the Father.

> *By myself I can do nothing; I judge only as I hear, and my judgment is just, for I seek not to please myself but him who sent me.* (Jn 5:19-23, 30)

A quick reading of these words might lead us to agree with the Jews' conclusion. Jesus claimed to share God's power, justice and honor. Wasn't he insisting on equality with God? Actually this passage can legitimately be interpreted as supporting the doctrine of the Trinity. But if we read it looking only for doctrinal proofs, we may very well miss its literary power. A closer reading will show that Jesus' words to the outraged Jews did not so much teach a theological truth as suggest a touching word picture.

If we *take time to visualize the picture the words paint*, we will realize that Jesus was not proudly proclaiming himself equal to God, but he was humbly acknowledging his total dependence on his Father. He related to God as a worshipful little boy, carefully watching his Father's every move and listening to his every word, doing just as his Father did and wanting nothing more than to please him. Perhaps as Jesus painted this word picture of his relationship with his heavenly Father, he was remembering the hours he spent as a child in Joseph's carpenter shop, learning a trade under his earthly father's guidance.

We know that our relationship with God can never be exactly like that of Jesus, God's only Son. Nevertheless, during Jesus' earthly ministry he made it clear that his followers could enjoy the same intimacy with God that he knew. He taught us to pray "our Father" with the assurance that "your Father knows what you need before you ask him" (Mt 6:8-9). He explained that his

Father's love for each of us is the kind of perceptive, protective love that an ideal earthly father would feel for each of his children.

> *"Are not two sparrows sold for a penny? Yet not one of them will fall to the ground apart from the will of your Father. And even the very hairs of your head are all numbered. So don't be afraid; you are worth more than many sparrows. (Mt 10:29-31)*

Paul also used family images to assure us we can lay all our human failings to rest in our intimate relationship with God.

> *Those who are led by the Spirit of God are sons of God. For you did not receive a spirit that makes you a slave again to fear, but you received the Spirit of sonship. And by him we cry, "Abba, Father." The Spirit himself testifies with our spirit that we are God's children. Now if we are children, then we are heirs—heirs of God and co-heirs with Christ, if indeed we share in his sufferings in order that we may also share in his glory. (Rom 8:14-17)*

This is a good place to point out that we need to *listen carefully to all the implications of the words God speaks to us in the Bible, not just the implications we find appealing.* When Jesus uses imagery to emphasize that we are God's children who are precious to, provided for and protected by him, we are glad to take this imagery to our hearts. But when Jesus' words suggest that our relationship to God should be that of adoring, obedient children eager to please their father, we may not be so anxious to apply his words to our own lives. When Paul assures us that we are co-heirs of Christ who will share in his glory, we listen gladly. We should be equally open to hearing Paul's reminder that we can expect to share in Christ's sufferings.

Jesus' Followers Belong to a New Family of Faith

Both Jesus and Paul used family images not only to picture the new relationship believers would have with God, but also to portray the new love and fellowship they would experience with their fellow Christians. Jesus assured his disciples that though they might have to sacrifice much to follow him, they would be rewarded with a new family, not just in eternity but in this present life.

"No one who has left home or brothers or sisters or mother or father or children or fields for me and the gospel will fail to receive a hundred times as much in this present age. (Mk 10:29-30)

In Paul's letters we find beautiful descriptions of this new family that is God's gift to all Christians.

You are all sons of God through faith in Christ Jesus. . . . There is neither Jew nor Greek, slave nor free, male nor female, for you are all one in Christ Jesus. If you belong to Christ, then you are Abraham's seed, and heirs according to the promise. (Gal 3:26-29)

Now in Christ Jesus you who once were far away have been brought near through the blood of Christ. . . . For through him we both have access to the Father by one Spirit.

Consequently, you are no longer foreigners and aliens, but fellow citizens with God's people and members of God's household. (Eph 2:13, 18-19)

Paul not only gave us word pictures of the family of faith; he shared very personally what belonging to this family meant to him. He clearly treasured the fellowship and support of his brothers and sisters in Christ. Perhaps nowhere does this come through more clearly than in the epistle to the Philippians, where Paul expresses his gratitude for Timothy his "son" and Epaphroditus his "brother," and for all the Philippians, "my brothers, you whom I love and long for, my joy and crown, . . . dear friends!" (Phil 4:1).

However, the joys of sharing in the family of faith were mingled with responsibilities. To convey the nature of these responsibilities, Paul often used images of parental concern.

We were gentle among you, like a mother caring for her little children. We loved you so much that we were delighted to share with you not only the gospel of God but our lives as well, because you had become so dear to us. . . . For you know that we dealt with each of you as a father deals with his own children, encouraging, comforting and urging you to live lives worthy of God, who calls you into his kingdom and glory. (1 Thess 2:7-12)

Sometimes for Paul, loving his brothers and sisters in Christ brought him great pain.

I plead with you, brothers, become like me, for I became like you. . . . My dear children, for whom I am again in the pains of childbirth until Christ is formed in you, how I wish I could be with you now and change my tone, because I am perplexed about you! (Gal 4:12, 19-20)

Reading Paul's vivid pictures of what life is like in the family of faith, we need to *be honest about our emotional reactions to the words* he uses. Perhaps we find in ourselves a longing for the unity, the closeness and depth of involvement his language conveys. But we may have to admit that there is a part of us that is made very uncomfortable by his words. Are we quite ready to surrender all the worldly distinctions of race and social status and sex that give us a sense of identity and may help us feel superior to others? Are we more than a little frightened by the demands, the responsibilities, the possible pain that close relationships in the family of faith may bring? Honestly tuning in to our emotional responses to the language of the Bible can teach us a lot about ourselves and the changes

God wants to make in us.

Effective Reading Is Subjective Reading

In chapter four we recognized that reading the literary language of the Bible is essentially a creative process. We must experiment with various approaches to discover which ones enable a passage to speak forcefully to us. In effect we engage in a personal dialog with the text, questioning it and letting it question us not just intellectually but on imaginative and emotional levels.

We can be moved by the imagery, drama and analogies of the Bible only when we ask questions like the following:

☐ How do I visualize (or hear, smell, touch or taste) what is being portrayed here?

☐ What rich associations and nuances do the words carry?

☐ What is my honest emotional response to the imagery or drama?

☐ What personal memories or longings do the words evoke in me?

☐ What tones of voice do I hear behind the words of the writer or the people in his story?

☐ Can I put myself in the place of the people I am reading about and imagine what they felt?

☐ Can I imagine how the original audience responded to the words I am now reading?

☐ Do the word pictures remind me of conditions in my own world?

☐ Where in the passage do I see myself?

☐ Do the images or dramatic scenes challenge me to change?

Not every question will apply to every biblical passage we read, but such questions will unlock the power of the Bible's literary language for us. Even as we ask these questions, however, we must remind ourselves that they do not have right and wrong answers. Our responses will necessarily be subjective. Paying attention to context and consulting historical reference books can help keep our interpretations on track. Nevertheless, in the process of opening ourselves to the power of literary language in Scripture, we unavoidably put that language at the mercy of our own personal experiences, emotions and egos to some extent.

We can see the problems this raises. In responding to images of God as Father, for example, won't we inevitably call up memories of our childhood experiences with our own fathers? One of my friends has taught me a lot about how to enjoy reading the Bible, for she is highly intuitive and responsive to literary language. Unfortunately, she had alcoholic parents. When we compare notes on how Bible passages portraying God as a father affect us, it's clear that pictures of God's righteous parental anger resound too loudly for her, while images of God's tender love have a hard time penetrating her wounded heart.

I have the opposite handicap, if you can call it that. Since I am the youngest of four children and the only daughter of a father whose life has always revolved around his family, the word *father* holds only warm, pleasant associations for me. It is easy to tune in to all the verses in Scripture that picture God as an affectionate, protective parent who showers his children with unconditional love and forgiveness. It is harder for me to hear and take seriously the passages that emphasize God's expectations of his children and how disappointed he is when they fail to obey him. I tend to assume God will always coddle me rather than challenge me to grow up.

Not only our experiences as sons or daughters, but our experiences as siblings and as parents will inevitably color our responses to the Bible's family imagery. If our relationships with brothers and sisters have been distant or bitter, won't the New Testament references to brothers and sisters in the faith seem like empty clichés to us? If we have never had a child reject us and all our values, will we be able to fathom our heavenly Father's pain when we rebel against him?

Even if any of us had the breadth of experience and imaginative capacity to relate to the whole range of imagery and drama the Bible employs, our personal responses to the literary language could not always be trusted. We are sinful human beings with an amazing capacity to see what we want to see and hear what we want to hear. However, adopting one more guideline for our Bible reading can minimize the risks of misinterpretation and, at the same time, make far more of the literary power available to us. The final, crucial principle is this: *we should consistently read God's Word in the context of Christian community.*

Reading God's Word in God's Family

Our family of faith consists not only of the local congregation we belong to, but of the whole church family down through the centuries. With the guidance of the Holy Spirit, this community of believers has been reading and interpreting the biblical text for almost two thousand years.

We can place ourselves in the stream of this ongoing tradition by listening to sermons and reading books on the Bible. Preachers and writers have been trained, as most lay people have not, in the broad sweep of Scripture, in the history of the church, and in the disciplines of theology and ethics. Their interpretations keep us on track when our subjective reactions would lead us astray. Furthermore, where our own imaginative responses to biblical stories and pictures would be weak and impoverished, their insights frequently open up new vistas of understanding for us. In a sense, when we listen to what the "experts" have to say about Scripture, we are connecting with a great cloud of witnesses who can guide us as we journey deeper into God's Word.

We can also meet regularly with a small group to study God's Word. In a group we will find the Bible taking on life and power far beyond what we could experience on our own. When an image of God as Father is encountered in such a group, people who have had different experiences with earthly fathers and are at different places in their relationship with their heavenly Father can share, compare and learn from one another's responses.

Even more important, members of a small group can provide the listening ear, the comforting hug, or the stern voice of rebuke when it is needed. In such a family atmosphere, God can be with us again in the flesh, letting us experience tangible expressions of his love through the concrete caring of other Christians.

As the Isaiah passages that opened this chapter remind us, we are all little children. Knowing how small, helpless and earthbound we are, our heavenly Father has found wonderful ways to reach out to us with his love. He entered into our humanity in the person of his Son. He speaks our language in his inspired Word. And he makes us part of a family, his household of faith, in which we can grow.

In order to unlock the power of Scripture, we do need to read the language of the Bible very personally. Once we discover all the ways biblical imagery, drama and analogy can touch us directly, we will come to Scripture with new excitement and confidence. This does not mean, however, that we can read the Bible on our own. If we depend solely on our individual responses, we will miss the guidance and support God wants to give us when we read his Word in his family. Only when we open our whole selves—heart, mind, soul and strength—to Scripture *and* to one another will God be able to draw us close and grow us up as he desires.

A Father and Two Sons:

A Bible Study Focused on Imagery of Family Relationships

Luke 15:11-32

Please note: This study deals with the parable of the prodigal son, one of the most familiar passages in Scripture. You will be asking your own questions of the passage so that it can speak to you personally with fresh power. Refer to the section "Effective Reading Is Subjective Reading" in the last chapter for ideas of questions you might want to ask.

1. Read Luke 15:11-32 aloud from three different versions of the Bible.

2. The sets of verses below divide the parable into separate scenes. Focus on each portion of the parable, each separate scene, as the story unfolds. First, think of two or three questions you could ask of each set of verses that would help you better understand the power of the scene. Then enter into a dialog with the story by answering the questions you raised.

a. Luke 15:11-13

b. Luke 15:14-19

c. Luke 15:20-24

d. Luke 15:25-32

3. Where did you see yourself in this parable?

4. Is there a particular message (this may be in the form of a picture, a feeling, an insight, a command) which you feel God has given you as you have reread this familiar passage? Write out that message to yourself. How do you feel God wants you to respond?

Appendix: Using This Book in a Group

How can you get the maximum benefit from *Unlocking the Power of God's Word*? Study it in your small group. In learning to respond to the Bible's literary language, you will be exercising some imaginative muscles which have probably grown slack through disuse. Any exercise program can be a bit intimidating, and it is always more fun to "shape up" with group support and encouragement.

The study questions in this book are ideal for stimulating lively discussion and significant sharing in a group. Because literary language is aimed at our personal feelings and experiences, group participants who are learning to respond to such language will be learning about one another at deeper levels than a more objective, analytical approach to Scripture might allow.

Here are some practical suggestions for using this book in a small group:

1. Move through the book in sequence, covering one chapter and its accompanying Bible study in each session.

2. Allow an hour or more for discussion of each Bible study.

3. Be sure you have at least three different versions of the Bible available in your meetings. Various translations handle literary language differently; one may be better for one passage, one for another.

4. Do not feel you need to cover all the questions in each study. Focus on the ones that will work best in your group. If some questions are helpful but too personal for discussion, suggest that members individually write down the answers to these questions, but always give an opportunity for people to share what they have written if they want to.

5. If your group is larger than five or six people, try splitting into groups of three to five for discussions. This gives more people a chance to share, and more of the questions can be covered in less time. When the smaller groups get back together, have a representative from each one share with the large group some of the special insights their small group discovered.

Two Possible Approaches Your group may decide between one of two basically different approaches in studying this book. If they are willing to do homework, all members can be asked to prepare for each session by reading one chapter. They may want to do the Bible study that follows the chapter as part of their homework, bringing their answers to the group meeting. Or they may want to save the study questions to discuss spontaneously as a group. This approach does not demand extra work on the part of the group leader, and leadership can easily be rotated from week to week.

Your group may prefer not to do homework. If this is the case, greater demands will be made on the group leader, who will be the only one to read the chapters. At the beginning of each session, the leader will need to summarize for the group the principles taught in the chapter. It may be helpful to read brief excerpts from the book. Then the group can proceed to discuss the questions in the Bible study. This approach will work better if your group does not rotate leadership.

Whichever approach you choose, expect to grow in your knowledge of God, of yourself and of one another as your group learns to unlock the power of God's Word.

Notes

Chapter 2: Letting God's Language Move Us
[1]Roy Pinney, *The Animals in the Bible* (New York: Chilton, 1964), pp. 93-95.

Chapter 3: Context Channels Our Responses
[1]Derek Kidner, *Psalms 1—72* (Downers Grove, Ill.: InterVarsity Press, 1973), pp. 165-67.
[2]See also Job 7:12; Psalm 89:9-10; 104:5-9; and Isaiah 51:9-10.
[3]Otto Boecher, "Water, Lake, Sea, Well, River," in *The New International Dictionary of New Testament Theology*, ed. Colin Brown (Grand Rapids, Mich.: Zondervan, 1975-1978), 3:984-85.
[4]Kidner, *Psalms 1—72*, p. 175.

Chapter 5: Bridging the Historical-Cultural Chasm
[1]"Turn! Turn! Turn!" from the album *Turn! Turn! Turn!*, recorded by the Byrds (Melody Trail, Inc., 1965). The words are from the book of Ecclesiastes, with adaptation and music by Pete Seeger.
[2]Clearly the first-century Jews had strayed far from the understanding of "chosenness" which was taught in Deuteronomy 10:15-19:

> The LORD set his affection on your forefathers and loved them, and he chose you, their descendants, above all the nations, as it is today. Circumcise your hearts, therefore, and do not be stiff-necked any longer. For the LORD . . . shows no partiality and accepts no bribes. He defends the cause of the fatherless and the widow, and loves the alien, giving him food and clothing. And you are to love those who are aliens, for you yourselves were aliens in Egypt.

[3]At times in the Old Testament the deaths of godly men such as Abraham and Job are presented as good and natural—they die "at a good old age" and "full of years" (Gen 25:8; Job 42:17). The New Testament writers also depart at times from the pattern of death equalling punishment and separation from God. In fact, the death of Jesus is pictured as good news, and New Testament writers often use images of death in a positive light in view of what Jesus accomplished on the cross.
[4]Roland de Vaux, *Ancient Israel* (New York: McGraw-Hill, 1961), p. 59.
[5]Among reference books I recommend are Henri Daniel-Rops, *Daily Life in the Time of Jesus* (Ann Arbor, Mich.: Servant Publications, 1962); Alfred Edersheim, *The Life and Times of Jesus the Messiah* (Grand Rapids, Mich.: Eerdmans, 1971); and J. A. Thompson, *Handbook of Life in Bible Times* (Downers Grove, Ill.: InterVarsity Press, 1986).

Chapter 6: Rediscovering the Drama Behind Doctrine
[1]George Eldon Ladd, *A Theology of the New Testament* (Grand Rapids, Mich.: Eerdmans, 1974), p. 182.
[2]In the book of John this incident takes place the day before the triumphal entry, but in

Matthew and Mark it occurs during Passion week. In either case, it contributes to the mood of ceremony that pervades the last days before Jesus' death.

[3]Old Testament sacrifice was not the only metaphor God gave the early church to help them understand Jesus' death. The concept of justification was drawn from the law court, and the concept of redemption was taken from the world of commerce. But sacrifice was probably the most vivid and pervasive metaphor, as John Stott explains in *The Cross of Christ* (Downers Grove, Ill.: InterVarsity Press, 1986), especially p. 168.

[4]See Matthew 26:1-5. Jesus died during the Passover Feast, as God willed, even though those who plotted his death intended that he should not die during the festival.

[5]Martin Hengel in *The Atonement*, trans. John Bowden (Philadelphia, Pa.: Fortress, 1981), and Frances M. Young in *Sacrifice and the Death of Christ* (Philadelphia, Pa.: Westminster, 1975) both stress that specific traditions in the pagan world of Jesus' time would have prepared the Gentiles to understand Jesus' death as sacrifice.

Chapter 7: Powerful Language Puts Us on Trial

[1]Allison A. Trites, in *The New Testament Concept of Witness* (Cambridge: Cambridge University Press, 1977), gives a good sense of the kind of court proceedings that are reflected in the Old Testament. See especially pp. 21-22.

[2]The term *gave them over* in verses 24, 26 and 28 is a forensic one. In Greek it is the same word used by John when the Jews "hand Jesus over" to Pilate for judgment and punishment in John 18:30.

[3]Trites, *New Testament Concept*, pp. 83-84. Her contention is that since witnesses do appear against Jesus in Matthew and Mark, it would seem that John purposely omits witnesses to emphasize the sense that Jesus has won his case by silencing his opponents.

[4]See the accounts of Peter and John before the Sanhedrin (Acts 4:5-12), Stephen before the Sanhedrin (Acts 6:12—7:51), Paul before a meeting of the Areopagus (Acts 17:18-31) and after his arrest in Jerusalem (Acts 21:33—22:21).

[5]See Acts 23:11, where Jesus comes to Paul to tell him he must testify in Rome.

Chapter 8: Reading God's Word in God's Family

[1]See Romans 4:13, 16; Galatians 3:14, 29; James 1:1; 1 Peter 2:9-10.

[2]See John 11:41-42. The only time we know of when Jesus addressed God more formally was in his cry from the cross, "My God, my God, why have you forsaken me?" (Mt 27:46), and that cry reflected the momentary abandonment by God which Christ had to experience when he took on himself the penalty for human sin.

[3]Otfried Hofius, "Father," in *The New International Dictionary of New Testament Theology*, ed. Colin Brown (Grand Rapids, Mich.: Zondervan, 1975-78), 1:620. Jesus' use of the term *abba* is indicated in Mark 14:36; Romans 8:15; and Galatians 4:6.